The Agony of Socialism:
Kazakh Memoirs of the Soviet Past

The Agony of Socialism:
Kazakh Memoirs of the Soviet Past

Garifolla Yesim

English translation edited by R. Charles Weller,
with assistance from Sheri Six

Asia Research Associates
Pullman, WA, USA
2017

English Translation © 2017 – Garifolla Yesim
Kazakh and Russian Editions © 2012 – Garifolla Yesim

All Rights Reserved. Apart from limited quotations,
this work should not be reproduced, in whole or in part, in any form,
without the express written consent of the publisher.

Printed in the United States of America

First Edition
First Print Release, March 2017

Asia Research Associates
525 Karcio Court
Pullman, WA 99163 USA
Telephone: (814) 327-7955
Email: ara@world-hcrc.com
Website: www.world-hcrc.com

ISBN: 978-0-9794957-1-7 (softcover edition)
Library of Congress Control Number: 2017934588

Special thanks to G.K. Shalabaeva, Director of the A. Kasteev State Museum of Arts (Almaty, Kazakhstan) for permission to use, throughout the book, the various images provided courtesy of the museum.

Cover picture: Unknown artist's rendering of Vladimir Lenin.
Courtesy of the A. Kasteev State Museum of Arts (Almaty, Kazakhstan).

Dedicated to future world leaders.

The Kazakh social and political philosopher, academic and politician, Garifolla Yesim herein brings *The Agony of Socialism* to light. Through narrative prose, the author establishes a connection between the theoretical concepts of Socialism and the (auto)biographical stories which put them into practice. Socialism is not a utopia; it is the lives of millions of people, their fates and their fortunes. Their stories are told through memoirs and essays that leave an unforgettable impression, compelling readers to think about socialist systems and to empathize with the people who have lived and still live within them.

****

Garifolla Yesim's little book is an insightful and deeply disturbing account of his upbringing and life in Soviet Kazakhstan and the process by which he reached his damning conclusions on Soviet socialism itself. Displaying his gifts as a writer on every page, he intersperses personal impressions with moving vignettes of actual citizens of Soviet Kazakhstan and the often horrific travails they endured. There is another side to all this, of course, but never again can we think of Soviet rule in that vast Central Asian land without being mindful, too, of this toxic heritage.

– S. Fredrick Starr, Chairman of the Central Asia-Caucasus Institute and Silk Road Studies Program, Institute for Security and Development Policy, and Research Professor at the Paul H. Nitze School of Advanced International Studies, Johns Hopkins University)

Garifolla Yesim's memoir of Soviet rule in Kazakhstan is a valuable addition to the literature about and by survivors of war, genocide, and totalitarian rule imposed in the name of ideologies of both the Left and Right. *The Agony of Socialism* uniquely blends the personal experiences of ordinary Kazakhs in the Soviet Union with reflections on the political theory and philosophy that framed and legitimized what was, at its core, a profoundly inhumane and unjust system. It at once speaks to the universal lessons of the human cost when states and parties dehumanize those under their control, and provides a rare window into the specific history and memory of Soviet rule in Central Asia, a subject that is virtually unknown, and inaccessible, to a general western audience.

– Raymond Sun, Associate Professor of modern German and European history, Washington State University

CONTENTS

Editorial Preface 1

Author's Preface 5

Chapter 1: Socialism and Me 7

Chapter 2: The Specter that Haunted Europe 73

Chapter 3: Collapse of the Socialist Camp 85

Chapter 4: What Did Socialism Give to the Kazakhs? 109

Chapter 5: Socialism and Its Shadow 137

Conclusion 145

Bibliography and Recommended Reading 151

EDITORIAL PREFACE

Amid continuing debate in the early 21st century, in the former Soviet states, the West, China and elsewhere, over the alleged merits and demerits of socialism as a political system, this work aims to expose its dark sides as experienced by the Kazakh (and other former Soviet) peoples during the Soviet era. The author, Garifolla Yesim,[1] was born (1947) and raised in Soviet socialist Kazakhstan, emerging thereafter as a top national academic and Kazakhstani senate deputy in the post-Soviet period. Drawing on his many long years of personal life and political experience as well as academic training, he weaves together a compelling narrative interspersed with his own insightful commentary and the real-life stories of those who endured the tragedies he has preserved through oral transmission and now bequeaths as a memoir for this and all future generations to carefully ponder.

I will not attempt here to provide an in-depth, technical introduction to Yesim's work. I will instead highlight only a few key issues in passing. First, Yesim makes several points within the main narrative which reflect one of several aims he has in publishing this work, in the original Kazakh (2012) and Russian (2013) versions as well as now this English translation. Deep into chapter one, after recounting numerous tragedies, he laments that

> [s]o many human lives were ruined, mutilated; so many souls disappeared in the giant millstone of the Soviet regime, when the mask of justice covered cruelty and violence. ...Little gods of the new power set their rules everywhere, eradicating the free spirits from everyone and everywhere. People lived in hell while dreaming of a heavenly life for their children.

Then, continuing this thread elsewhere, he says: "The Socialist regime came to power and destroyed the Kazakh way of life." He, likewise, explains how

> Communism came to Kazakhstan through forced and missionary means. At first, we learned of Communism at gunpoint. Then when the repressions started, we accepted it out of fear, and thus, we became Communists. ...it is very hard to erase the ideas of Socialism and Communism from memory, because they can change form and reappear and successfully thrive in our lives.

Elsewhere he says: "It is not easy to erase the ideas of Communism and Socialism from the mind. That may be the reason why Communists have lately begun to actively intervene in and try to influence some political events. It would be inexcusable to underestimate them."

---

[1] Yesim has also been transliterated as Esim, on the internet and elsewhere.

Among other things, Yesim carries a concern for certain influential figures within Kazakhstan today who still hold to and advocate a socialist-communist perspective. His Conclusion thus begins: "The wider the chasm grows between the rich and the poor, the more the nostalgia for Socialism appears." Earlier in chapter one, he warns: "All the playing with Socialist ideas led to severe social turmoil. Those who come after us need to understand and recognize that." At the start of chapter five, he likewise says:

> Conversations about Socialism's history still continue, and I believe they will not quiet down anytime soon. People are looking for a way out of the world financial crisis, and for some reason, they circle back to the idea of Socialism, to the legacy of Karl Marx. It is a very dangerous route, fraught with consequences.

His book aims to convince them, and anyone else entertaining such ideas, of this danger and its consequences. He is also concerned with how "the young generations who have been born in other times, who have never experienced the pressure of Socialism's propaganda" will view its past history. Indeed, he declares in the Conclusion that "I dedicate my novel to you," the Kazakh youth who will lead the country in years to come.

But Yesim addresses another historical, and seemingly personal, problem as well, one raised by the lingering 'specter of socialism', when he says:

> The greatest bitterness is that many people, honest and pure in heart, believed in the ideas of Socialism. ...Are we who once lived under Socialism to blame? If so, what should be our redemption? Perhaps, we can console ourselves by asserting the inevitability of fate? If the guilt does not escalate to a crime, is forgiveness then possible? What about those who committed crimes—how do they live on? There are no specific and precise answers to these questions.

Two of the foremost answers Yesim does offer to the dilemmas posed by Socialism, however, are cited from the nineteenth-century Kazakh national poet Abai Kunanbaiuhli (1845-1904): "Love all of humankind as fellow kin" and "[l]ove fairness and equity, as these are the path of truth." In light of many who choose 'an eye for an eye', it seems an apt, even noble response to the suffering and inequity experienced by those whose stories Yesim tells.

Whatever other aims and concerns Yesim may have, his memoir raises complex questions of 'history and memory', recounting as it does, many long decades later, both his own and various other personal experiences in the Soviet past. Indeed, as Geoffrey Cubitt points out, in a 2007 book titled *History and*

Memory, "memory has become" over the past quarter century or so "one of the central preoccupations of historical scholarship." In connection to questions of oral, folk, and popular history, Cubitt includes within this preoccupation "efforts in the post-Soviet era to recover and to re-evaluate the pasts that Communist regimes had systematically suppressed." Within the study, Cubitt deals with both individual as well as collective memory and the intimate tie between them. Both are forms of "retrospective knowledge."[2]

In telling not only his own story, but others from the time, including select family members, Yesim wishes to codify and preserve what has heretofore been, due to the forbidding nature of Soviet historiography, passed on to him orally and visually from as far back as his youth. Indeed, the stories included reach from as far back as World War One down to the post-Soviet period. In reference to the Soviet obscuring of the past, Yesim says, in speaking of the 'Great Famine' under Stalin and Goloshchekin: "If even the illiterate elderly Beysen knew that the famine indeed took place, then the professor should know about it for sure. Why hadn't he told us about it? History was supposed to be about everything that had happened; there should be no secrets or allusions."

How much Yesim's representations of the past are, however, colored by lenses of the present are questions of 're-interpretation' and 're-imagining' which are difficult to answer. Certainly a critical reading of his account is in order. Yesim himself says, "I will not claim that everything I know about Socialism is the ultimate truth. As the saying goes, every mountain has its peak; and my stories are only words, uttered by me." I nonetheless concur with professor Raymond Sun who, in drawing from his own studies of Holocaust survivor accounts, considers Yesim's contribution "a valuable addition to the literature about and by survivors of war, genocide, and totalitarian rule" which "provides a rare window into the specific history and memory of Soviet rule in Central Asia, a subject that is virtually unknown, and inaccessible, to a general western audience."

R. Charles Weller
Washington State University (History)
and Georgetown University (ACMCU)

---

[2] Geoffrey Cubitt, *History and Memory* (Manchester, England: Manchester University Press, 2007), pp. 1-2, 134-135. See also: Jacques Le Goff, *History and Memory*, tr. S. Rendall and E. Claman (New York: Columbia University Press, 1992) and J. M. Black, *The Holocaust: History and Memory* (Bloomington, IN: Indiana University Press, 2016).

AUTHOR'S PREFACE

When I think about my past, I understand that my entire life was leading me to this novel. Everything I wrote about, everything I talked about, it all touched upon the topic of Socialism. It could not have happened any other way. I was born in Soviet Central Asia under Socialism; I grew up and matured into adulthood during those times.

Socialism is our yesterday, our past, our lives spent. That is its value. I see Socialism the way many other people do—it is part of my biography. It is part of the history of Kazakhstan, and history should be valued and preserved.

Socialism penetrated into Russia from Europe and was forcibly instituted in Kazakhstan. Socialism was engendered by a desire for a fair social system. Time proved it to be an adverse experiment. But science teaches us that a negative result is still a result. In this context, Socialism is the result of a search for fairness and equity. In this memoir, I talk about the fates of people who lived in Soviet Kazakhstan during the time of Socialism. I come from the generation that was destined to live in that time. Part of my story is, therefore, included.

This narrative about Socialism will leave no one impassive or indifferent. A visceral response is natural because it is impossible to ignore or overlook our socialist past. Socialism is a universal subject for all mankind to contemplate.

CHAPTER 1
SOCIALISM AND ME

Socialism is a subject that I know very well. I was born during Socialism's reign in Soviet Central Asia; I lived in a Socialist society for forty-four years. I have studied the theory of Socialism for many years and have engaged in propagating its ideas among the people. On this occasion, a colorful expression comes to my mind, "You can live in Paris your entire life, but still not know it." I will not claim that everything I know about Socialism is the ultimate truth. As the saying goes, every mountain has its peak; and my stories are only words, uttered by me.

I will start from the beginning.

I was born on April 15, 1947, into the family of a poor man. At that time, Socialism had already settled deep into the Kazakh land. The Great Patriotic War (World War II) had ended only two years before. Life was just starting to turn around in the nomadic villages.[3] Life was hard, hungry, and cold, with no clothing or shoes, or even a full meal. But propaganda and ideology were in full swing. It became a tradition to glorify Joseph Stalin and chant praises to him in every key.

At that time, Kazakhstan was called the Kazakh Soviet Socialist Republic and was part of the Union of Soviet Socialist Republics (USSR). Moscow was the capital of the Union, and the main nation was Russia. Russification spread everywhere; it was mandatory for everyone to know Russian. Soviet Party officials were teaching children in Russian schools; generally all the intellectuals of that time belonged to the Party. Kazakh schools were mainly in villages. Other than boarding schools there were no Kazakh schools in the cities, and all Kazakh schools taught in Russian. In this way Socialism solved the problem of the nationalities policy.

There is no one who has not been a child. As the years go by, memories become livelier and clearer; they suddenly appear, like secret documents from archives. Ever since my childhood, two realities have been imprinted in my memory. The first is the festive atmosphere, with

---

[3] EN (Editor's note): The Kazakh word behind 'village' is 'aul', which can mean either a nomadic encampment or the later conversion of these nomadic encampments to sedentary agricultural villages via Stalin's collectivization program. The latter still retained elements of semi-nomadic herding lifestyle, including the practice of 'zhailau' – summer pasture.

red flags and streamers everywhere and columns of demonstrators. The second is hunger.

We were not just cold and hungry, we also did not have any clothes. All my peers and I were tortured by questions of what to wear to school, how to get school uniforms. Here is one of my memories of that time.

My Story

The 1950s were hard times for many people. My half-starved childhood is embedded in my memory, and nothing can erase it.

I am in second grade, and I live in a district center with my distant relatives. My parents work in a *kolkhoz* (Soviet collective farm) sixty kilometers away. The owner of the house, K, is a combat veteran missing one leg, one arm, and one eye. Every month he gets a pension of thirty rubles,[4] which has to feed the entire family. There is no other income. His wife does not work and stays home all day long. They have four children, two boys and two girls, and then me. It is not enough to say that we lived in poverty. It would be more accurate to say that we lived next door to starving. We only got a proper meal when my parents would come from the kolkhoz, bringing meat, butter, oatmeal, and *kashk* (yogurt) balls. But that joy was short-lived; the food would disappear as fast as snow under the sun, and then we would have to go back to our half-starved life.

Every hunger has its mystery, its secrets. Only those who have experienced starvation can imagine what hunger really is. For example, it is much easier to play outside when you are hungry than it is to fall asleep with an empty belly. I toss and turn deep into the night, stomach growling and gnawing, until I finally surrender to sleep, and it is always the same dream that comes: I dream about a loaf of white bread.

---

[4] EN: For clarification of the value of the ruble at this time, see *1955 Ruble-Dollar Price Ratios for Intermediate Products and Services in the USSR and the US* (Washington DC: Central Intelligence Agency, 1960). (URL:
https://www.cia.gov/library/readingroom/docs/DOC_0000326151.pdf)

The Agony of Socialism

"Celebration on a State Collective Farm," A. Kasteev, 1937. The painting displays, in propagandistic style, the joyous mixing of Kazakh traditional and Soviet industrial life. As revealed by Yesim's memoir, behind the celebrations was a significant measure of hardship and sorrow. Indeed, the painting was done right in the middle of Stalin's 'Great Purge' (1936-38). Courtesy of the A. Kasteev State Museum of Arts, Almaty, Kazakhstan.

The neighbor kid Sergey, Matvey's son, always brings a loaf out to the yard. I pretend to play with him, but I am drooling. Sergey breaks off a piece for me. I feel like I do not even chew, but swallow it whole. As soon as it reaches my mouth, the bread disappears, like air. Sometimes I purposely stay home to avoid meeting Sergey and taking his bread.

K's son, Beybit, is the same age as me. Beybit does not do well in school; he is especially poor at penmanship. Once, after looking at my notebooks and gradebook, K started scolding Beybit. He got so angry that he beat him. The next day, Beybit brought home another 2 (2 was the failing grade in Soviet schools), and K beat him again. After that, K calmed down, but every time Beybit got another 2, he would shoot a disapproving look at me.

Beybit's mother took a dislike to me as well. During meal times, she would ostentatiously put the best pieces on her sons' plates. Beybit would still be loudly slurping his soup when, having finished my meager portion, I would thank her and move away from the table.

One time K noticed. "Hey, woman, don't play favorites. Feed them all the same," he snapped, digging her in the ribs with an elbow.

As the days went by though, I learned that nothing would change about the food distribution. I eagerly awaited the holidays, when I would come home and would forget about food. Instead, I would spend all day long swimming in the lake and playing with neighborhood kids till dusk.

But the holidays were still a long ways away. Now I was sitting and looking longingly at my boots. They had been new in the fall, but by the middle of winter, they were a pitiful sight.

When you chase a piece of ice on the freshly frozen Irtysh River, passing it to others, or when you dig out some tin can with the toes of your boots and kick it up with a bang, do you really think about the need to take care of your boots?

I cursed myself up and down and forgot all about my empty stomach; instead, I dreamed about a pair of new tarpaulin boots. At that time they were the ultimate dream for every boy, especially if they had a felt insole inside and warm foot wraps—Oh my! Then your feet were on fire, no frost was too cold. You could tie on skates, grab onto a passing sleigh, and go for a fun ride.

I sighed and decided to stitch up the hole in my boot somehow, so I started looking for an awl. K noticed and said, "I'll patch that up properly tonight. Get ready now. You'll come with me to the store to buy boots."

My heart leaped with joy. My parents must have sent some money for boots, but then why did he want to patch up my old ones?

It was bitterly cold outside, so we walked quickly to the store. "Find the kid some boots," said K.

The salesclerk placed a few pairs on the counter. "What are you waiting for? Try them on," he said.

The boots were a good fit; I took a little walk around in them, feeling on top of the world.

"OK, that's enough. Take them off," K said suddenly.

"But they fit him just right," the salesclerk tried to argue.

I also started to say that they were a perfect fit, but K interrupted me.

"My friend," he said to the salesclerk, "I'm not buying the boots for him; they're for my son. His foot is one size smaller. Understand?"

I stood there, thunderstruck. In complete silence, K counted out the money as the salesclerk put boots, one size smaller, on the counter. A lump rose in my throat; I heaved a quavering sigh and realized that I was shaking all over.

"What are you standing there for? Let's go," K's voice brought me out of my daze. I realized that he had only brought me so his son would not have to go outside in such cold weather.

Back at the house, Beybit put on his boots and joyfully walked around the rooms, and no one told him "that's enough." I just sat, back in my usual spot in the corner, and started on my homework, and every letter that I carefully drew in my penmanship notebook was near and dear to me.

Reflections

My understanding of Socialism started with Vladimir Ilyich Lenin. At school, we had to memorize many poems about Lenin. When we became Little Octobrists, a Communist youth organization, we wore a star-shaped pin with Lenin's picture in the star's center, on our chests. We swore oaths to live by Lenin's principles. I decided to learn as much as possible about Lenin, so I started reading books about him. I really liked his slogan "Learn, learn, and learn." Learning was so much fun! I wanted to be intelligent like Lenin. In our family circle, however, I heard other opinions about him.

My understanding of the world was based on a system of persuasions, which were mutually exclusive at times, and on ideas that were diametrically opposed. The school would say one thing, but the village elders and my family would say the opposite. I remember that all conversations at the table were open, no one paid attention to the kids listening in; I actually thought they wanted me to know their opinions. During the evening tea and deep into the night, they talked about the nation, its history, its heroes—Ablai Khan, Kabanbay batyr, Bogenbay batyr. I never heard the names of the Party leaders from their lips; they called Stalin, "the Mustache," and Nikita Khrushchev, "Baldy."

I remember one incident that happened in the fifties. It was not a significant event, just one episode that got stuck in my memory, one statement. For many years that statement, lodged in my brain, was a riddle, wrapped in an enigma. Only now has its meaning become clear.

That evening, the villagers and relatives who had come to say hello to Grandpa Yesim stayed late at the table. The conversation was about politics. At that time, people were having a lively discussion about a serious concern: Nikita Khrushchev (r. 1953-64) had just given a speech denouncing Stalin (known as the "Secret Speech"); the downfall of the Stalinist regime had begun. Some supported Stalin's dethroning; others did not. I knew that my grandpa was against the Mustache, but he did not welcome Baldy either.

My Story

Grandpa did not know the modern alphabet, so he made me read the paper aloud. I tried to read about Khrushchev's decree emphatically, making my voice sound solemn and pompous.

"Ah, this one won't last long, either," Grandpa said after my reading. I paid no attention to his words and went on with my recitation.

I finished reading and put my head on Grandpa's right shoulder. He handed me a paper, "Here, read what else he is saying." I went on reading with emotion, as best I could, inserting pauses and emphasizing some words. I did not understand the meaning of many words. Judging from the adult's reactions, they did.

Baldy was talking about private ownership, which Communism would supposedly abolish. All people would live with free food and housing.

"Say what you will, but he is doing a great job. Private ownership is really only a yoke around your neck," the ever-drunk Kaplanbek said.

"Now it seems that the Soviet government is for loafers and lazybones, who only eat, drink, and lay around, and here I thought that it was the government for the deprived," that was what the history teacher, Sagat, said. He was an intelligent Communist and a veteran who had gone through the entire war and had come back alive, but with bad lungs.

Uncle Sagat always surprised me. He was a teacher, a Communist, but he was always opposed to everything the Communists wrote in the papers. Once I heard him translate some article from the

Communist newspaper, *Pravda* (Truth), into Kazakh and conclude, "Aqsaqal ('white beard', i.e. respected elder), this is a most deceitful paper." The teacher's words had sent a chill down my back. After all, I was anxiously awaiting the day that I could read that paper with ease.

The night was getting late and people started heading home. "What can I say? The government that is created through deception will perish by deceit," Uncle Sagat said angrily, then gasped for air in a fit of coughing.

"Watch out, Sagatzhan,[5] you're in the public service," my grandpa warned him, but he did not question or contradict him. I, however, was unhappy with my grandpa's actions. Why didn't he tell Uncle Sagat that he was wrong? How can a teacher be against the "Truth" newspaper? My history teacher praised Khrushchev to high heaven, often citing *Pravda*. I thought it would be curious to know what Uncle Sagat told his students.

Uncle Sagat did not live long after that. He died at the end of the 1950s. People from the district committee could not find his Party membership card, no matter how long they looked.

For many, it was a mystery. But I remembered the teacher's words, "the government that is created through deception will perish by deceit," and I understood why the membership card could not be found.

Reflections

The Soviet ideology took its toll, and my judgments were gradually molded in accordance with the general atmosphere, which differed from the opinions of my grandpa and Uncle Seit. I became a Young Pioneer, a Soviet youth organization loosely based on the scouting organization model, and proudly tied their symbol, the red kerchief, around my neck. Later, I joined the Communist Youth League (Komsomol), and became an active member in that political organization.

Socialism took up a solid position in my mind. During my second year at the Semipalatinsk (Semey) Teacher Training College, where I was a straight-A student, I was accepted into the Communist Party. I had two complaints against Socialism. The first was the starvation I had to endure as a child; the second—a

---

[5] EN: 'Zhan' appended to a name in this manner means 'my dear', thus 'Sagatzhan' is 'my dear Sagat'. Some names, however, contain 'zhan' as part of the full proper name.

hard life, resource shortages, and any other problems—*I attributed to the troubled postwar years and to bureaucracy. But when I picked up* Pravda, *I would sometimes remember the words of my maternal uncle, Sagat, "Let me read you a paper in which every word is a lie," and he would read* Pravda, *translating it into Kazakh, and doubt would creep into my heart.*

Kamal's Story

Even after so many years I[6] can still hear the cheerful shout of Samat.

"Wake up! Wake up, Kamal! They're already here, right there! Hurry up!"

Those dreadful years have paled into oblivion, but go figure. It seems like it was easier to survive them than it does to reminisce about them now. So much aimless anger and pain burn through me when memories of the past flash before my eyes. It is overwhelming to think of how people could have endured and suffered through it all.

The only thing beyond human power is resurrection after death; people can survive everything but death. With each torment we suffered through, another was waiting in the wings. We drained the cup of sorrow to the dregs. How many happy possibilities never came into being? I am talking about the hundreds of young people whose lives were lost before they had a chance to bloom. How could we grieve and mourn those who were lost? We could not cast a handful of soil onto their graves because they did not have graves—no one knew where they laid their bodies to rest. We could only wish for one thing, that it would not happen again.[7]

My poor Samat. He was so happy to see visitors then, so full of joy. If only we could have known how it would end.

At that time Samat was thirteen, and he was an excellent artist.

---

[6] EN: The first person within each of the stories is not Yesim, but the person whose story Yesim is telling, in this case Kamal.

[7] EN: This reference, the remaining story, and several subsequent stories, are about the famine experienced across many parts of the Soviet Union in the early 1930s, especially in the grain producing areas, particularly Kazakhstan and Ukraine. Later in the chapter it is refered to as "the Great Famine." See esp. Robert Conquest, *The Harvest of Sorrow: Soviet Collectivization and the Terror-Famine* (Oxford University Press, 1987); Valerii Mikhajlov, *The Great Disaster: Genocide of the Kazakhs*, tr. K. Judelson (Stacey International Publishers, 2013); and Anne Applebaum, *Red Famine: Stalin's War on Ukraine* (Doubleday, 2017).

We had no paper, so he would smooth sand in one swift motion then draw our profiles. When we would go into the woods, he would carve portraits of kids from the village on birch trunks. He would also draw us on doors and windows, but those he would erase right away to avoid getting scolded by adults. We would crowd around him and beg him to save the drawings. He would smile, and shuffle his feet, and promise us, "You just wait; when I get lots of paper and paint, I'll make portraits for all of you."

So we looked forward to the time when he would get the necessary supplies.

Samat was a sharp kid, full of energy. He had an immense desire for anything new.

He was the first to know all the village news, and he would report it to us. Maybe because we were the same age, he would take me everywhere with him. But I had one weakness that sometimes frustrated my restless and quick pal. I loved to sleep. If I had a free moment, I would fall asleep right away. "Come on, sleepyhead, don't be such a lazy bum," Samat would sometimes rail at me. But I would not bat an eyelid, snoring on unworriedly.

The day the visitors arrived, I had taken our only cow to the glade. When I got back home, I covered myself up to my ears with an old fur jacket and indulged in my favorite pastime.

"Wake up, wake up! Come on, hurry!" Samat shook me awake and pulled me outside, still half asleep.

"There, see that dust," he pointed at the road leading to the district.

"So what?" I was puzzled. "It's probably hunters coming for some game, or the horsemen are breaking in a horse."

Realizing that I did not understand, Samat said hurriedly, "No, it's Goloshchekin, the chairman of the regional committee. He and Lenin defeated Tsar Nikolas, and he's a close friend of Stalin."

I looked at him. His cheeks glowed, and his eyes were alight. I just shrugged my shoulders as if to say, "So what, we hear that every day." Everyone knew of Filipp Goloshchekin.

The car with Goloshchekin passed by without stopping at our villages's administration building and went on to another village. It was the first time we had seen a car, and it left clouds of dust behind as it flew down the new road. "Too bad they didn't stop here," Samat said disappointedly.

I found out the reason for his disappointment later. It turned out that he had secretly drawn portraits of Stalin and Goloshchekin, and he wanted to give them to Goloshchekin in person. Samat was sure that Goloshchekin, pleased by the gift, would ask what he could give him in return. Then Samat would ask for art supplies so he could make all our portraits.

Our village administrators were upset that they did not get to personally shake Goloshchekin's hand and decided to take it out on us. As he was passing by us, Chief Zhanpeis suddenly lashed Samat with a whip. "You brat! Go tell your father to come to my office."

Whenever Zhanpeis caught sight of children, he became furious for some reason. The village children would scatter as soon as they saw him. However, we had been busy watching the car and had not noticed him approaching. Samat was hit by the whip, but I managed to jump away.

Chairman Zhanpeis had a reason to go after Samat first; he had old scores to settle with Samat's father, who was the village teacher. Samat's father was an intelligent and knowledgeable man, and many people would come to him for protection from Zhanpeis. People said the teacher had high-ranking friends in Almaty (at that time known as Alma-Ata, capitol of the Kazakh Soviet Socialist Republic), which was why even the chairman was a little afraid of him.

However, there were a lot of rumors about the teacher in the village. They said that he had not outlived his feudal vestiges, that he had a second wife in the district center, and even that he was a Japanese spy. From my older sister, Asiya, I knew who was spreading such rumors. They all came from Zhanpeis, who had decided to get rid of the teacher no matter what the cost.

When the teacher was called to the administration office, he quickly dressed and went there. He was gone for a long time. Samat and I were running in the yard, pretending to be playing, but we were secretly keeping a close eye on the road. Samat suddenly stopped, sighed heavily, and sat down on a timber block that was used for a chair, "Kamal, I am scared of that monster, Zhanpeis. There are all kinds of rumors about my father."

"Don't be afraid; he can't do anything. Your father has many friends in Almaty. They'll defend him if something happens."

As soon as I had uttered those words, Samat's eyes filled with tears and he jumped up.

I was surprised and confused and just kept asking, "What happened? What is it?"

After a while, Samat wiped his tears and forced himself to smile, "Yes, yes, Dad has many friends in Almaty." Later I found out that, around that time, many of his father's friends had been arrested.

"Dad!" Samat saw his father and ran to him. The teacher looked terrible. He had turned white; his face was pale as paper. There was no anger or bitterness in his eyes, only detachment and emptiness. He hugged Samat, kissed him on the top of his head and told me, "Kamalzhan, tell your dad..." he paused, clearing his throat. "Tell Kaseke to come to my house. We need to talk."

My father was downhearted when he returned from the teacher's house. My mother and he were whispering about something long into the night. At one point, my dad woke me up and asked me to go get my uncle, my mother's brother.

In the morning, my *nagashi*'s (maternal relative) voice woke me up. He trumpeted, "Where would we find that? It's outright theft! Do they want to kill us, or what?"

As it happened, my nagashi was soon dead. In the years of famine, he and a dozen other families decided to move away to Altai, but someone must have blown the whistle on them. They were caught and beaten up, and my nagashi died of his injuries. The children straggled away, and we never knew what happened to them. I heard that one of them lived in Barnvillage, but he did nothing to find his relatives and became a stranger.

Early that morning, I found out why the family had stayed up all night.

"Strengthen working discipline in collective farms" – Tashkent, Uzbekistan, 1933 (Mardjani Foundation). Soviet propaganda poster. Source: Wikipedia, "Collectivization in the Soviet Union." Image: Public Domain.

My mother grumbled from the kitchen, "I hope you rot. This is no gift; they just took everything the other day."

Indeed, a few days ago, Seitkul had come limping over and took the required grain delivery away on a wagon. I did not understand what more he needed.

I got dressed and went outside. Of course, Seitkul was not alone. Next to him was Chairman Zhanpeis, Samat's father, some stranger in a hat (who turned out to be the commissioner), and my father. My poor dad was confused. He fumbled with his hat, glanced at Zhanpeis and the commissioner, and tried to explain something to them.

But no one, apart from Samat's father, was listening to him. Eventually Zhanpeis lost his patience and grunted with discontent, "Kaseke, you are a smart and rational man. If you don't understand, then who will understand the Party line. The commissioner, here, thinks that, following our nation's hospitable traditions of gifting visitors, we should send a valuable present to Chairman Goloshchekin. If we do not support this initiative, then we are worth nothing. By sending this present, our kolkhoz will exceed its required grain delivery, which will be proof of our devotion to the Party."

At that, Zhanpeis looked at the commissioner, as if making sure he had said it right. That man nodded in a portentous manner, "Father, Chairman Zhanpeis knows what he is doing," he uttered slowly in measured tones.

"You will leave us with nothing, and winter is coming. What is going to happen to us?" my dad said obviously giving in.

Samat's father stayed quiet, but we could see he was ready to explode. The commissioner cast angry glances at Zhanpeis. My father recognized the warning in those glances and started walking toward our storehouse, calling, "Hey, gimp, grab a bag and follow me."

Seitkul pretended not to hear what my father had called him; he jumped from the cart, grabbed a metal stick, a kind of poker, and hobbled after my father.

My dad tried to outwit them. He pulled out three bags of grain at once, saying those were his last ones. He thought that, if they took any, they would probably take only one.

But I knew we had more grain; we had packed seven or eight bags from the harvest. My dad and mom were happy then, saying "Thank God. Now we don't have to fear the winter." Now those bags, which were their hope, had to be given away as a gift.

Certain his trick had worked, my father said, "This is all we have. If you want to drain us dry, take it all, leave nothing, but I think one bag should be enough for a gift."

Seitkul felt that Zhanpeis was annoyed by my father's words, so he started poking the dirt floor of the entryway. I saw my father's face grow pale and realized that a disaster was about to happen. I thought, "Why did he have to call Seitkul a gimp?"

Seitkul poked the metal cane, which was hollow, into the ground and inspected its end very closely each time he pulled it out. If there was grain in the ground, kernels would get stuck inside the metal tube. Standing in the far corner, Seitkul once again pulled out his poker, and a few kernels fell out of the hollow tube. Seitkul almost jumped with joy. His eyes gleamed as he looked at my father with an air of triumph.

The chairman glared at my father and hissed, "You could get exiled from the kolkhoz for concealing grain, but Comrade

Commissioner forgives you this time," and he looked at the man in a hat, as if asking for confirmation. The commissioner nodded very subtly. Then Zhanpeis ordered Seitkul, "Take the grain bags out and load them up."

The commissioner seemed satisfied with such an outcome and pronounced, "Comrades, we still have a lot of houses; hurry up and finish here." Limping, Seitkul haltingly pulled the bags to the cart.

Zhanpeis shot a look at my petrified father, "Kaseke, do not worry; we did not see that you hid grain. But we commend you for gifting three bags of grain to Goloshchekin of your own free will." The commissioner nodded importantly in confirmation.

In this way, Zhana Talap kolkhoz gifted Goloshchekin an additional seventy poods (over one ton) of grain. Endless tears were shed, countless damnations were sent after the collectors. Below the signatures of the chairman and the commissioner, the telegram said that the people had offered the grain surplus of their own accord.

The satisfied commissioner had carried two documents in his briefcase. One concerned the delivery of grain; the other was a denunciation of Samat's father. The second document determined not only the fate of the teacher, who was soon arrested, but it was also a gloomy omen of woes and ills to come for the entire village.

After the arrest, Chairman Zhanpeis did not hesitate. He moved Samat and his mother into a cramped old dugout, saying that the family of an enemy of the people did not deserve to live in a large house. The limping Seitkul moved into the teacher's house.

The village people, who had already turned in all their livestock to the state, began to starve, even before the winter came. Samat and his mother were the first to experience famine. Samat's father, in an attempt to appease the administrators, had given them all their stored grain.

My father filled half a bag of wheat and told me to take it to Samat. When I entered their dugout, I did not recognize Samat's mother, she was so gaunt and withered. Samat rushed to me, hugging me and bursting into tears. His mother started crying too. The three of us sat quietly crying, hoping to God no one would hear and report us for crying because we were unsatisfied with Soviet power.

A few days later, my family, for reasons unknown to me and not due to production necessity, was sent to a winter hut about fifteen kilometers away from the village. My father began shepherding the kolkhoz livestock. Life at the winter hut was actually easier; at least we managed to milk a cup or two for ourselves and drink it away from prying eyes.

The winter brought a lot of snow. Every day our dugout door would be buried in snow, so my mother could not get out to milk the cows. Often, she would wake me up and the two of us would get the door open.

One morning, I pushed the door, but the snow seemed tamped, and the door would not budge. I kept pushing at the door, and when I finally got it open a few inches, I climbed outside and began to shovel the snow. Suddenly, my shovel hit somebody's clothes in the snow. I backed away and ran back into the house in fear. I woke up my father, and the two of us dug out the unfortunate person.

It was Samat. Poor Samat must have gotten desperate and decided to come to us, but he did not make it, did not have enough strength. At least that was what my father said later, when we mourned my poor friend late into the night. My father went to the kolkhoz to tell Samat's mother of her son's death, but she had gone mad. She did not come to her son's funeral.

That winter the farmers of Zhana Talap kolkhoz almost died of famine. Some left their homes, headed deep into the Altai region, and found their final resting place on the road; others swelled from hunger and died at home. By the fall of 1932, fewer than fifteen households had survived.

I have been carrying this heavy load inside me for many years. Now I have shared it with you, but the pain has not diminished; only my grave may bring me peace. I thank heaven that at least I now have the opportunity to talk about that time.

But I can still hear Samat's joyful call, "Wake up! Wake up, Kamal! They're getting closer. Here they are, right here, very close already!"

If we could have only known that the moment portended a storm of grief for the kolkhoz. But neither Samat nor I were suspicious of anything, and we stood on the side of the road watching the car disappear into a cloud of dust.

It amazes me: I went through the turbulent years of collectivization in the thirties. I saw famine and death. But it is a hundredfold harder, even unbearable, to recall the past. It seems that it was easier to survive all the horrors than it is to remember them now. I only close my eyes, and my memory obligingly digs up one or another image of the old days. Then, an incredible pain strikes me and fills my heart with rage and fury. A man can survive anything, adapt to anything, and get accustomed to anything; the only thing that he cannot do is resurrect from death.

Reflections

Kamal's story planted doubt in my heart. I was crushed by the burden of questions that had no answers. I thought, "How can I believe that our country is the best after everything I have heard?"

During the winter holidays, I came home and visited my Aunt Ayken. I asked her to tell me about herself, about all her life experience.

"I see that you won't leave me alone," she said. "Very well then, I will tell you. Although Grandpa Kosym probably told you most of this already during the long talks the two of you shared."

"No, Apa (aunt), he told me that I should hear it all from you; he did not tell me anything."

"All right, but just keep in mind that I'm not the only one involved in this story, and it is much more complicated than it seems. Why reopen old sores? It's all in the past and long forgotten. What's the use? Everyone wants to know all about the old days now. It may be right, who knows. I'm just afraid that bad times may come again."

"Auntie, we just need the truth to restore justice, that's all."

Aunt Ayken's Story

Our parents had three of us. My father was a diligent, hard worker, a peasant of average welfare. He was caught up in a confiscation: two or three cows, a horse, and about ten sheep became property of the kolkhoz and were handed out to the poor, while he was exiled from the kolkhoz. In one day, my mom was left alone with three children, without her husband or any means of support. She often said that she, or rather her beauty, was the reason for all the misfortunes that fell upon the family.

There was a man named Kalen, who had some power; he noticed my mother and made advances toward her. She turned him down. So the beast held a grudge and filed accusations against my father. Now, many years later, I do not know if it was my mother's fault, but I remember the immenseness of her grief and the weight of the load she had to bear.

When father was exiled, our relatives' visits grew fewer and farther between. My older brother, Yerbol, got tuberculosis, and in a few days he was gone. The shepherd Sapar was the only one to bury him. Soon my second brother died too, and I was sick.

My mom was frantic with grief and fear for me, her only child still alive, and went to her family. I remember her sitting before her parents, sniffling with tears, and saying that she would not survive if I died.

For a whole month, I was given hot melted marmot fat. I did not expect to ever experience an ordeal harder than my illness. But in 1931, a dark cloud of famine descended upon us. It is impossible to describe what happens to people when they are starving. It can only be compared, perhaps, to total insanity. We somehow scraped by until spring. By some unknown means, my mother had procured a bag of millet; she begrudged every kernel and gave me strict orders not to talk about it with anyone at all. But she was a very kind and warmhearted woman, so ultimately it was my mother who gave away the secret.

We lived privately and quietly. One day came after another, all alike, as peas in a pod. There were no more rejoicings, songs, or festive feasts. Every day brought news more frightening than the last. When my mother would find out that someone had died of starvation, she would grow pale and stiff. Before bed, she would check the bag of millet to make sure it was still in its place, and with that comfort, she would sleep. In the middle of the night, she would get up and go check the bag again. Later I figured out the reason for her worry.

People, desperate because of their powerlessness and hopelessness, may commit the most improbable and terrible acts, driven by an instinct for self-preservation.

Human nature is revealed in moments of utmost happiness or in critical situations. Famine, for instance, may make a person forget everything humane.

I witnessed that with my own eyes when I was fourteen. Back then I was too hungry and weak to be surprised at people's behavior, because starvation dulled all feelings.

We had a neighbor, Myltykbay, who had many children. Even in good times their lives were not easy, but in the year of famine, they became the first victims. The oldest one, sixteen-year-old Konyrbay, was accused of stealing and was badly beaten by someone in the village; he died at the gate of his house.

Their daughter Marzhan had been weak, feeble, and sickly from birth. She became the first one to die of famine in our village. We had been friends and had often played together. Mom broke down and, on the day of Marzhan's death, she called Myltykbay's wife over and, with shaking hands, poured her a bowl of millet. Even now, many years later, my mind can see that same image: my mother's shaking hands pouring millet for Myltykbay's wife.

My poor mother must have sensed disaster coming. In her mind, she understood that she should not have exposed our secret. After all, what could a bowl of millet do for a crowd of hungry and sick kids? But she could not refuse her heart.

The next day Myltykbay's wife came over again. Mom poured her more millet, but said something in a quiet voice. When the neighbor came by a third time, my mom refused her. Though I was half-asleep, I remember that she pointed at me and argued passionately with our neighbor.

Myltykbay's wife hung her head and started to shuffle away, but she stopped at the threshold, turned around and said, "Zhamal, I would not come to you on my own. It is your *qaynag'a* (husband's oldest brother); he went completely crazy. You should hide your bag better or else trouble will find you. They say people have started eating human flesh." As soon as she left, my mother and I tried to hide the bag. We went through the entire house, but no matter where we thought to hide the ill-fated bag, it always seemed like it would be easily found.

At a loss, we hugged and cried for a long time. Suddenly, my mother wiped her tears, got up, looked at me sternly and said, "There is no use crying. It does no good. We need to do something. Bring me small bags; we'll fill them up with millet and hide them in the pillows." I was content with my mother's idea, but when I started pouring the last of our millet into a small bag, she stopped me.

"Leave some millet in original bag. That fiend won't calm down until he finds our food."

The next day, Myltykbay's wife died. That evening, Myltykbay kicked in our door and started yelling at my mother. His eyes were bloodshot and he foamed at the mouth as he threatened and insulted my mother, demanding that she give up the millet.

"Your boyfriend with the torn lip will bring you more. He's ready to give the shirt off his back just to sleep with a woman. You have nothing to lose. Share your loot with me, or it will get much worse."

The so-called boyfriend with a torn lip was that very same Kalen who had reported my father.

My mother listened to the neighbor calmly; then, leaning on me, she got up with difficulty and said, "Let us die of hunger, so you, jackal, can live." At that, she threw the bag with the remaining millet at Myltykbay's feet. Then she fell to her knees, put her face in her hands, and wept.

Standing silently, Myltykbay glared at her. Finally, he grabbed the bag and said, "Just you wait, bitch, I'll get you," and staggered out.

My mother got up and came over to me. She kissed me and said that father would come home soon; then everything would be all right. "I was not able to save two of our children. If something happens to you, how can I look your father in the face? When your father returns, Myltykbay will not dare to stand up to him. He acts all high and mighty now, but he is only taking advantage of your father's absence. We just have to put up with it."

As I listened to my mother, I thought of Yerbol. Oh, if only he were still alive that scoundrel Myltykbay would not have dared step through our door. As if she had guessed my thoughts, Mom sighed, "Yerbol would have been seventeen this year."

I do not know how long we sat there holding each other in the dark. Then my mother got up, "That damned Myltykbay made me forget. I brought you some meat today." At that, she pulled out a small bundle from under the covers. There was a piece of meat in it. Real meat! We could not remember the last time we had eaten meat. Soon, the pot was boiling and the aroma of cooking meat filled the house. When the food was ready, Mom pulled out a big slice of bread from somewhere. I looked at it suspiciously. Where did all this wealth come from? My mom noticed my glance and said, "Remember your father's Russian friend, Matvey (i.e. Matthew)? I met him today. It turns out he knows everything about us. He's the one who has given us meat and bread. He promised to drop off a bag of flour in the fall too."

That night, we stayed at the table for a long time. We remembered the past, told some fun stories. I praised my father's friend, though I did not recall ever meeting him.

My mother had a wonderful red dress. She took it out of the chest and put it on. I ran across the room and kissed her saying, "I have such a beautiful mom."

But by morning our joyfulness was gone. Another of Myltykbay's children had died of hunger. People started trying to move south, where wheat was available. Kalen, the commissioner, the one that Myltykbay was talking about, was chasing them all around the steppe forcing them back into their villages.

Each day, while my mother was at work, I stayed home with the door locked, anxiously awaiting her return. Incidents of cannibalism were becoming more frequent. One day she came home earlier than usual. Without taking off her overcoat, she fell flat onto the bed, shuddering and crying for a long time. It seems that someone had written an anonymous letter to the kolkhoz chairman complaining that the wife of an enemy of the people (my father) was working in the kolkhoz.

The terrified chairman replaced my mother with a woman from a group of new settlers. At that moment, I felt that starvation was standing at our door. Then another trouble came. As soon as the sun went down, Myltykbay tried to force his way through the door, "Hey, bitch! Open the door or I'll chop it into bits with my axe." To emphasize his point, he banged his axe on the doorjamb.

"He's not going to go away. We'll have to let him in," said my mother.

As soon as she opened the door, Myltykbay stormed in, pushed my mother out of the way, and headed toward me. "Don't try to stop me, bitch. Your daughter is in her prime. I'll either make her my woman or get some fresh meat out of her. We're all going to die anyway, but you will die before me." With that, he grabbed my arm and pulled me toward the door. Mother fell at his feet.

"I am begging you! For Heaven's sake, don't touch my daughter, my blood and soul." She grabbed Myltykbay's boots, trying to stop him. Myltykbay hit her on the back with the axe head and, in a frenzy, he kicked her as she lay at his feet. In a fit of despair, my mother ignored the pain and kept begging the fiend, "At least wait till tomorrow; I will bring her over to you myself in the morning. Let me say good-bye to her, pack her things. You have a mother, too—you understand, don't you?"

"Tomorrow, who knows what will happen tomorrow. I may kick the bucket overnight."

Then my mother jumped up, ran to the bed, ripped open the pillows and started throwing bags of millet toward him.

Myltykbay calmed down, picked up the bags, and said, "All right, have it your way. But if you whisper even a word to anyone, you'll regret it. Nothing will stop me."

When our torturer left, we tried to lock the door, but it turned out he had locked us in.

We hurriedly packed some clothes and belongings and what food we had left. We broke the window and, trying to avoid being seen, we ran down the road leading to the city.

"I bear no guilt before your father, daughter. Now we need to get to the city. We'll find some work there and hopefully some shelter."

We reached the city in two days. For a long while, we tried to visit relatives, asking to stay overnight, but the answer was always no. The last one we visited, the old Nuridin, shook his head and said, "It is a good thing that you saved your daughter, my dear. She can stay with us. As long as I am alive, I won't let anyone hurt her. However, we don't have much; you can see that. You are young. You can find a way to make a living for yourself. I'm sorry, sweetheart, but that is my decision."

"Ata (father, grandfather, respected elder), thank you. I do not need more. Let me just visit her sometimes. I'm sure I can find some work in the city."

"Oh, my dear, it's hard to find any work now. But you are a clever woman; you will think of something."

That was the start of my life in the house of Aqsaqal Nuridin, who was my father's uncle. They were good and kindhearted people. Their son, who was a loader at the dock, was the breadwinner. Sometimes my mother stopped by; she was pale, with dark circles under her eyes, and her face was swollen from hunger. Then suddenly she disappeared for a whole week.

One day, Nuridin-ata found my mother, early in the morning at the gate of the house, with no traces of life. "She could not make it and starved to death," Nuridin-ata said as he closed her eyes. "Her body is still warm, Grandma. Take care of her."

I had no tears. We put my mom in the entryway and prepared her body properly. I hugged my poor mother's head and clung to her. I did not know how long I stayed that way, until I heard Grandma say, "Grandpa, take her away. The poor thing is scared, and I am afraid her heart may stop." But evil chance seldom comes alone. As soon as we buried my mom, Grandpa's son got injured and took to a hospital bed. They said he had strained himself lifting up a heavy bag. Kasengazy (that was his name) spent a lot of time in the hospital, and then he was sent to a home for the disabled. Later he got married and started his own family.

Everything the old couple had saved for a rainy day disappeared in a flash. Now I had to take care of them. A person can put up with and get used to anything. The old woman kept telling me that I had to endure whatever happened and accept it. Soon I understood why the old woman hammered that into my head so persistently.

One day the house owner, a forty-year-old, spotted man, dragged me into the barn and raped me. Only then did I understand the meaning of the old woman's words. I clenched my teeth and submitted.

Eventually the spotted man's wife caught us together. Screaming and cursing, she grabbed my hair, pulled me outside the gate, and locked the door. But that was not enough for her. While I was standing in a daze, trying to decide what to do, the gate opened, and I saw her heading toward with me with a red-hot poker. I bolted from her, trying to avoid the poker. But she was determined to mutilate and cripple me.

"I'll make sure that no man will ever look at you again, you slut," she yelled, swinging her poker.

I have no idea how it would have ended if the man had not acted quickly; he snatched the poker out of his wife's hands and locked her in the house.

"I would rather die than step over the threshold of this house," I thought to myself and wandered off into nowhere. I lived on the street for a few days, spending the night wherever I happened to be with others who were homeless like me. We ate scraps. What happened later you probably know from Grandpa Kosym.

"It has been three years since Kosym-ata passed," Aunt Ayken said. "When he was alive, he would get angry if I started to talk about my past. I guess he did not want me to get upset. It is the other way around now; people have started talking openly about those times. If Kosym-ata lived to this day, he could have told so many stories."

Reflections

Yes, Kosym-ata (Grandfather Kosym) took the truth of those frightening hungry years to his grave, but he did tell me the story of Ayken-apa.

"Long time ago, in times immemorial, when our sons returned with a great victory, a great trouble started. That trouble had a menacing name: hunger."

I looked at him with surprise and tried to see if he was joking.

Kosym-ata squinted his eyes at me, and said, "You think it's strange that I want to tell you about a most frightful thing, but I start my story as if it were a fairy tale. My father died in those years. He did not die of starvation only. He was very ill, but he could not watch people suffering. He was what you now call a writer. He left a little chest of manuscripts; however relatives burned them for fear they might cause troubles. But people remember that he was a storyteller. They still say, 'That is what Seit said.'

"Before his death, he called me over, joking and laughing. In the end, he said, 'Son, just give it time; the moment of truth will come. Then you will remember the past and start your story like this: A long time ago, in times immemorial... Our life is a fairy tale and not the truth. Somebody's imagination and amusement created our life. The great truth has not been told yet, but when it is, no one will believe that we survived through that time. It will seem mythical and improbable. That is why I tell the stories of the past like a fairy tale.'

"Those were my father's words, may he rest in peace.

"So now I am saying good-bye to life, but I did not see the great truth come. That is why my life is also a fairy tale."

Kosym-ata, indeed, did not make it to today, when we can talk about everything openly, with no fear. Here is one of his stories of the past.

Grandfather Kosym's Story

A long time ago, we lived in the city. Father was a loader at the dock, and I was a general worker in the meat factory. I was seventeen. One day my father and I went to the market to get some groceries. It took us a while to shop around and bargain, and finally we bought half a bag of potatoes and hurried home. At the market entrance we witnessed this scene.

I should say that in those years there were a lot of dead people on the streets. We were so used to it that we sometimes even stepped over a body without really noticing it. There was a special burial team that picked up the bodies and buried them outside the city. They dragged the dead people into one pile, and then stacked them into a cart.

As one of the burial team men grabbed the legs of yet another victim, my father suddenly called out, "Don't touch that child!" and he ran over to the body. It was a girl about thirteen years old. Her dress had slipped up, exposing her hunger-bitten body. Father pushed away the gravedigger and carefully lifted the girl up; he was about to place her body on the cart when he noticed that she was still breathing; he immediately turned and carried her back to where I was standing.

"Hey, old man," the nearby policeman shouted at my father, "put that body back on the cart."

"She is still breathing; this girl is alive. I'll take her home with us; she may live."

"Drop her. If she is not dead yet, she will be on the way there or when they bury her."

"You animal! They should bury you instead of this child," my father yelled, his eyes shooting fire.

"So that's what you think. Then take that. Here's what you get for calling me an animal...Take that! And that!" The fat policeman started lashing my father with a whip. Forgetting about my own safety, I rushed at him, snatching the whip out of his hand and throwing it away.

"You just wait; I'll see you both rot in prison," the fat man spit through his teeth.

"Before you throw me in prison, I'll wash your face with your own blood, right here! Go away before it's too late," my father said, enunciating every word and looking straight into the policeman's eyes. Then we picked up our half bag of potatoes and, with the girl in our arms, we went home.

To make a long story short, mother nursed the girl back to life and health. You may have already guessed that this girl was Grandma Ayken, mother of your friends Askar and Bolat. When the girl came to herself, she told Kosym and his wife everything. They went to see Nuridin, but it was too late: both he and his old wife lay dead at home. They had no one to bury them. The dentist, Nurym, who often comes over, is the grandson of Nuridin and the son of Kasengazy.

Grandpa Kosym grew quiet, buried in thought.

Reflections

My memory has preserved these stories told by the adults.

In 2011, Ayken-apa passed away. As she liked to say, "Every path and road is buried in dust."

Are these really just long-forgotten bygones, as Kosym-ata said in his story introduction? Should I keep the story of Ayken-apa in my memory? I have no answers. But it is true that this terrible disaster happened. It is also true that many stories are buried deep in oblivion.

When we were kids, we memorized many verses that we liked for their measured rhythm; they were easy to remember, their meaning was simple and clear.

For some reason, one of them comes to my mind more often than others. It was a poem by a famous poet, titled "Turksib."

I remember that it glorified the hard work of the people who had built the railroad. The poem had these lines:

> *The bitter sweat that flows down,*
> *It breaks the rock and mills the stone.*

Now these images bring horror. But as children, could we feel their true, sinister meaning? It was not the stones being crushed, not the mountains being broken, it was the human souls being milled under a giant press.

But we were kids, and we chanted cheerfully and vibrantly:

> *The bitter sweat that flows down,*
> *It breaks the rock and mills the stone.*

Now I ruefully recall those years, and I pity myself. There are many reasons for that, and I begin to understand everything only now. My memory about those years brings up one of the elderly Beysen's stories.

The Elderly Beysen's Story

The old woman had a crazed look, her hair always disheveled and sticking out from under a headscarf. For some reason everyone called here Turksib-apa. She never caught my attention, and every time I met her, I passed by with no concern for her.

I remember though that whenever my mother saw the old woman, she would slip a bundle with some food or clothes into my hands and tell me, "Son, run and give it to that poor woman. Allah will reward you, and she will bless you, too." But the old woman never showed any gratitude. She only gazed into my eyes and asked, "Have you seen Ayman or Sholpan? Have you seen them? Come on, tell me."

When I told my mother about that, she wiped her tears with a corner of her scarf and explained, "Poor unfortunate woman. Those were her two daughters. She had two daughters, Ayman and Sholpan."

I did not know why my mother would get so upset when the conversation drifted around to the crazy old lady. I never had time to ask, so this mystery remained unsolved for me for many years. Time passed, and slowly life was turning around. The stores started offering not only meat and butter but even halva and sausage.

You hardly ever saw beggars asking for alms anymore. People said that the authorities had put them all together into one house, and they lived there with free room and board. Turksib-apa had probably been in such an institution when she disappeared from our village for a long time. Then, recently, she showed up again.

Her route was well known; she usually wandered along the railway tracks, weaving back and forth across them. She had no fear of being run over by a train. When they saw her, the engine men would signal her, and Turksib-apa would step off the tracks and wait for the train to pass, keeping her eyes on the wheels. It was always the same, summer or winter, and everyone was used to her habits and constant questions about Ayman and Sholpan.

Turksib-apa had no family here. She was not local. Her husband had died a long time ago. The old woman lived here with distant relatives. Truth be told, she did not live in a house, but in a little shed that was built specially for her. In winter, she fueled her own furnace and ate whatever she could find.

Most often, though, you could see her wandering on the train tracks. When it was bitter cold, the engine men would help her up into their boiler room. They would warm her up with tea and give her some food. She was of a mild and quiet nature; there was no person who would hurt her, refuse to let her in, or swear at her.

But my memory reaches back for one unpleasant experience. Ever since people had recovered from past disasters and life was getting better, their regard for her had become a bit frosty. The first herald of such attitudes was when some village villagers built decent houses and put a high fence around them.

Matvey and Kuspan outdid everyone by putting barbed wire around their fences. One of the respected aqsaqals of the village could not bear that, and he told them in a fit of temper, "No good will come of it, sons; remove the wire."

"Aqsaqal, those kids give us no peace. They have stolen all the tomatoes and cucumbers from the garden," they tried to explain, pointing at us. I did not know what else they said, but Kuspan and Matvey soon took the wire down. The wire was gone, but the chill in the relationships between people was growing.

A Soviet advertisement for the Moskvitch (and Volga) car. They were called 'Moskvitch' in honor of Moscow, the Soviet capital. The model referenced in the main text was from the 1950s or 60s (cf. the ref. to Khrushchev), most likely the small, compact size, one of the few models available to the broader population, in limited, monitored measure through application and approval. Photo credit: John Lloyd (flickr.com).

Soon, another remarkable event happened in the village: Kuspan bought a Moskvitch car. The car seemed like a wonder; it was all sparkling and gleaming.

I could only dream of getting to sit in that car, just for a little bit. Suddenly, my dream came true.

One day my mother pushed a small bundle into my hands and sent me to the crazy old woman again. On the way I met Sergey, Matvey's son, and asked him if he had seen Turksib-apa. Sergey smirked and pulled me toward Kuspan's house, "Come on, let's go. I'll show you Turksib-apa and something very interesting."

The owners must have been busy at dinner. The shiny Moskvitch was right there in the yard. Someone was in the car. I looked inside—Turksib-apa was sitting in the back seat looking for something, turning everything upside down. Sergey and I climbed into the front seats. I grabbed the wheel. I only wanted to steer a little, but I accidentally hit the horn. Furious, Kuspan dashed out of the house. He kicked us out of the car, cursing and taking swings at us.

We stopped a little ways off to watch what would happen with the old lady, who paid no attention to Kuspan and kept on looking for something.

"You hag, it's about time for you to go to your eternal rest, but you are still idling your life away. Get out of my car."

The old woman did not even glance at Kuspan. Enraged, he grabbed her by the shoulders, pulled her out of the car, and like in a boxing match, he punched her in the jaw. The poor woman flew backward and fell on the ground. Kuspan rushed over to continue his punishment, but his wife heard the shouting and ran to him, "Are you insane? Don't you see that she is a sick woman?" With that, she helped the old woman up and wiped off her blood.

We did not stick around to watch what happened afterward. We scurried away before we got in trouble. I never told anyone about what had happened, probably because I felt guilty.

Sergey could hardly hold back his tears and kept saying, "I feel sorry for the old woman; she did nothing wrong."

We walked back home in silence. I lied to my mother, saying that I could not find the old woman.

Yes, the past cannot be compared to anything. It is like a moment. It dashes by and is gone. Sometimes your whole life seems like one flash of lightning. I graduated from school, went on to college. Summer arrived, and I came back home for holidays. Nothing had changed in the village; everything had stayed the same. When I walked by Kuspan's house, I noticed that the fence that had once been solid, was now sagging, with rotten and warped boards. Through a hole in the fence, I looked into the yard. The Moskvitch was still there, but it was not shining with paint and nickel anymore; it was flaked and dented on the sides.

When I got home, my mother and father were upset by something. They exchanged a few words with me, and my mother said, as if apologizing, "Son, you are tired from the road; have some tea. Then go with your father to collect Turksib-apa. They say the poor thing died and is lying there on the railway bed." Then, with a habitual motion, she wiped her eyes with the corner of her scarf.

"Yes, have some tea. Meanwhile, I'll go talk to Kuspan about using his car because the *sovkhoz* (state farm) cars are at the thrashing floor," my father said, getting up.

I wanted to tell them about that incident from long ago, but I lost my nerve and stayed quiet. My father did not notice my hesitation and quickly left the room.

"The deceased had only one brother-in-law, but he moved away. He had forced her to leave with him, but she came back to us anyway, and she has been staying with us since then," my mother explained drying her tears.

I sat at the table, but I could not eat a morsel. I stepped outside and saw that my father was already getting into Kuspan's car and was calling me. I climbed into the back seat. We drove along the railway, and in about five or six kilometers, we saw a group of people.

"There, someone has already come," my father said.

"It's the railway men," Kuspan said. I stayed quiet. I felt incredibly weak. I had never seen a dead person before, and I was feeling queasy.

My father must have sensed my state. He turned to me and said, "There are people here to help; you should go back home, son."

He did not have to say it twice. I immediately jumped out of the car and flew home. I told my mother what was going on, and I attacked the food like a wolf.

"My poor son, those studies have consumed you completely. Look, your cheekbones are like razors; you can cut with them." With that, my mother hugged and kissed me. I looked up to see her eyes tearing up again.

"How come you are such a crybaby, Mom?" I joked.

"Son, every time I remember my twin sister and her horrible death, I just cannot stop my tears. The poor thing's mind was darkened from hunger or from despair. All she wanted to do was get a dead sparrow out of the well, and she drowned. I am amazed that I survived. I thank God for that."

It was the first story about the Great Famine that I had heard from her. I wondered what that famine was, and how something like that could happen during the Soviet times. The textbooks did not mention a word about it. Wasn't the entire history made only of victorious five-year plans? If the famine did happen, in which five-year term was it? Adults only gave evasive answers to my questions.

I counted to myself, "First five-year term, second five-year term, third five-year term... then the war came..."

In one history lecture, the associate professor, a short man with a round belly and a bald spot covering his whole head, was talking about the victorious advance of successive five-year terms with great gusto, when my classmate Serik, who was a bit older than all of us, suddenly interrupted him with a question, "Could you tell us, during which five-year term were the Kazakhs dying of starvation?" I remember the teacher, foaming at the mouth, came down on him like a storm cloud, "Who told you about that? Tell me!"

The entire village came to Turksib-apa's funeral. No one cried. Only my mother wiped her eyes a few times with the corner of her scarf.

After the funeral, everyone gathered at our house. The conversations drifted from one subject to another. Someone started talking about politics. Some praised Khrushchev, others cursed him up and down. Then, the talk switched to the old Turksib.

"What a dog's life. She won't even have anyone to read a prayer for her."

"Why didn't you notify her brother-in-law?"

"He's in a bad situation, too. Wasn't he the one who shot his only horse just so he wouldn't have to give it to the kolkhoz?"

"That's why he moved away from here."

"As soon as it started getting better for us, they took everything away again, without payment."

"Sure, hardly anyone liked that, but what could we do? We had to accept it."

Khismet, the recorder, who had recently moved into our village, asked, "Why was the old woman called Turksib-apa?"

The old aqsaqal let out a deep sigh, "Oh, Khismet, those were turbulent times, when we almost lost our selves, not just our names given to us at birth. I knew the poor woman when she was a young sister-in-law and had just come to our village. She was very handsome and graceful, and she had a ringing name that suited her well—Aysha.

I could not imagine that the old woman with disheveled hair was named Aysha. I remembered my classmate Aysha. She was what my mother called a raving beauty. Every time I saw her, I would break out in a sweat and blank out, losing every word. I think the girl must have guessed my feelings for her. But that was all right. I would find my way. I snuggled down and stared at the aqsaqal, hoping to hear Turksib-apa's story.

However, the conversation just would not start. Everyone was quiet and thinking about their own lives. I snuck a glance at my father. He did not show any interest for the topic. I looked at the others—it was the same.

It seemed that no one there intended to talk about the life of the old Turksib.

I worried that I would never find out the truth. Khismet was my only hope; if he did not make the old-timers talk about the old woman—that would be the end of that.

Khismet seemed to have read my mind and said, "So, aqsaqal, you said that the deceased was called Aysha?"

Khismet could not be ignored. He might have been a new person in the village, but he was a needed one. Ever since all the livestock was taken away, the only hope people had was their salary. Khismet was the one who ran the payroll calculations.

Aysha came from Pavlodar, from a small town called Arbigen. Her father was a known man of wealth in that area. He sensed the impending threat and decided to get his daughter off his hands as soon as he could. His son-in-law, Temirkozha, was a smart chap. He lived by transporting goods from China. But one time he did not return. He was either killed at the border, or he joined a gang. Some said he was a Chinese spy. Anyway, the man disappeared into nowhere.

Aysha had had a good life with her husband, but then she was left alone with her twin daughters, Ayman and Sholpan, and trouble rained down on her. Only God knows how much humiliation, pain, and suffering the poor woman, defenseless without a husband, had to endure. She was not the only one in that type of situation. At that time, there were so many widows and orphans who had no one to stand up for them; anyone who felt like it could offend them. Who could they complain to?

Who could they ask for protection?

It seemed to me it was then when some fearful timidity and resignation appeared in the nation. The need to survive at any cost forced people to obey implicitly, to be submissive executors of somebody else's will. Even when the better times came along... Well, once the people had slipped into that state, they found it was easier to live that way.

Just imagining those terrifying years gives me chills, but it had to be a hundred times scarier to experience them firsthand and go through all those hellish torments.

People, panicked with hunger, started eating each other. Aysha was horrified at the thought that her babies might be kidnapped. From despair and hopelessness, she decided to meet her demise, together with her daughters. Their house was close to the railroad. Aysha tied each girl's arms and legs together and laid down on the tracks with them. The terrified girls were screaming and crying from fear, but soon, all three went under the wheels of a passing train. Aysha was ready to die, but she must have bent her head lower in the last minute. When the train passed and everything grew quiet, only the girls had died. When Aysha opened her eyes, she faced a horrific image: her babies, her daughters, were lying in pools of blood, but she lived. God saved her life, but took her mind. Ever since then, Aysha walked the tracks like a lost soul, looking and calling for her dear daughters. After those dreadful years had passed, people started coming back to their senses. Kindness and sympathy for the pain and suffering of others returned, and everyone who saw Aysha considered it their duty to offer her food and water.

The young Aysha was gone. In her place was that old woman with deep lines in her face and grey straggly locks of hair waving in the breeze.

Soon her true name was forgotten. Everyone, young and old, started calling her Turksib-apa. That was the name she died with.

The elders sighed and said that, even if the soul of poor old Turksib would not get into heaven, she would definitely not end up in hell. They recited a requiem, said amen, and went home.

Reflections

Even though the elderly Beysen spoke slowly, with no haste, carefully choosing his words and pauses, there were a lot of things I did not understand. For instance, what was the famine? How did it start? How come there was no food all of the sudden? Where did the goods taken away from the 'bais' (wealthy peasants or herdsmen) go?

I went back to the city after the holidays. I consulted with Serik and decided to tell our history professor, who was teaching us the Party's history, about Turksib-apa. I wanted to get information about the famine from him. If even the illiterate elderly Beysen knew that the famine indeed took place, then the professor should know about it for sure. Why hadn't he told us about it? History was supposed to be about everything that had happened; there should be no secrets or allusions.

I only wanted to know the truth, to try and understand what had happened in the past, understand how such misfortune had come to the nation. I had no idea that we had some turbulent years ahead of us as well. It was the fall of 1969.

I know a person who witnessed the onset of the construction of Socialism. That person was my Grandfather Yesim. In 1914, when World War I started, he was drafted into the army. On the frontlines, the Kazakhs did not receive any weapons; they were sent to do support works, to dig trenches. People were discontent; riots started flaring up here and there. In Turgay, it was Amangeldy Imanov who led the riot; in the South, it was Bekbolat Ashekeyev. The national history called those events the national liberation movement.

The famous Kazakh author Mukhtar Auezov's novel **The Hard Times** tells about one such tragic event. Kerensky, the head of the provisional government, said there was no special need to draft Kazakhs for support works.

I questioned Grandpa Yesim for a long time about what had really happened. I wanted to know any details because I was trying to imagine what had actually taken place. One day, I think I was in the eighth grade then, Grandpa Yesim told me one story about a man called Alikhan. Back then I surely did not know what Alikhan he was talking about. Grandpa always said his name with respect and called him "the Torey" (descendent of Genghis Khan).

For me, a torey was an enemy of the people. We were taught that toreys were against Lenin. They subverted the Soviet government and wanted to destroy the Bolshevik regime.

Grandpa, on the other hand, talked about Alikhan Torey with great reverence. No one around argued with him or denied his words.

Even though I was hostile to the word torey, I enjoyed Grandpa's stories.

As a result of the tsar's order of 1916, Grandpa had been drafted and sent to dig trenches. The front was somewhere on the Minsk line at that time.

Grandpa Yesim's Story

The deployed were all young people. We dug trenches during the day and gathered in the barracks in the evening. We talked, sang songs, remembered home, tried to support each other. Most of us were from Semipalatinsk; others came from Aktyubinsk. We were divided into groups of tens, with a leader assigned to each group. I was the leader of my group. It was our responsibility to take care of the weak and the sick. Leaders also kept in touch with each other. Red-mustached Mikhail, our Russian envoy, knew about that and did not interfere in our doings. He had tiny, angry eyes and could speak excellent Kazakh. He seemed to have an informer among us, but we had nothing to fear—what secrets could we have?

Bogembai was the leader of the group from Ayagoz. He was built like a *bogatyr* (a brave and honorable knight), tall and broad-shouldered. He used to compete in sports. He also had a strong and beautiful voice, and he played the dombra very well. He was very kind and just.

We often had heart-to-heart talks, and he would always say, "You just wait, Yeseke.[8] I'll go back home, get married, and invite you to my wedding."

Bogembai's relative, Kasengazy, was one of his ten. He was feeble and frail, so he tired quickly and was often beat by the envoy. Mikhail would have put him in the grave long ago if it were not for Bogembai's patronage.

It happened over dinner. Amid the clinking of spoons and munching, there was a sudden commotion. As it happened, when his tablemate had stepped away for a minute, Kasengazy had quickly eaten all the tablemate's food. When the tablemate had returned to his spot and found his dinner gone, he lunged at Kasengazy and tried to strangle him. If it were not for Bogembai, the poor chap would have met his maker.

Bogembai got angry at his relative's reproachful conduct; he grabbed Kasengazy by the scruff and was about to swing his fist, when he

---

[8] EN: Here again is the 'ake/eke' ending appended to the author's name 'Yesim' in shortened form used to indicate a form of informal respect.

saw the Kasengazy's imploring look, his doleful eyes. Bogembai dropped his fist and said with sadness, "Shame on you, weakling," and stepped away.

Bogembai gave his dinner to Kasengazy's tablemate, who had been left without food. After that day, Bogembai started giving half of his food to Kasengazy, who would demolish it all without batting an eye.

It will come as no surprise that Kasengazy was the reason for his protector's death.

One evening after dinner, Bogembai slouched in his seat and played the dombra. We were tired and drowsy. At that moment Mikhail, the envoy, stormed into our tent, furious as a bull. "You bastards! You dare to sing," he lashed his whip a few times, hitting the backs men resting nearby.

Bogembai jumped up and pulled the whip out of Mikhail's hands.

"Mikhail, I asked you not to use your fists with us," he said angrily.

Mikhail quailed and immediately backed down, "Look, Bogembai, there will be trouble. I just counted—we are missing one crowbar."

The room grew quiet. Yes, Mikhail was right. The officer who handed the tools out to us, had warned, "It is your weapon. The soldier's weapon is a gun, yours is the crowbar. If the soldier loses his gun, it means summary execution for him. If someone loses his crowbar, he will get the same punishment."

Bogembai said, "Stay quiet. Now everyone grab your crowbar and line up." It was, of course, Kasengazy who did not have his bar.

"You idiot," Mikhail growled. He sprang up and started pounding Kasengazy.

We just stood there, not saying a word. What could we do? It was Kasengazy's fault. Finally, Bogembai could not take it anymore. He told the envoy, "Okay, that's enough."

"How can you say that, Bogembai? Don't you realize that they will send me to the front line now?"

Everybody understood. Kasengazy had left his crowbar in the trench that day. By evening, it had become the battle area. No one knew who was in the trench at that moment—our guys or the Germans.

Mikhail kicked at Kasengazy, who was sitting on the floor, "Go get your crowbar, you bastard." Kasengazy grabbed Mikhail's feet, crying and kissing the toes of his boots.

"You miserable thing, you can't even die with dignity," Bogembai snapped at him angrily. He threw the weeping Kasengazy in my direction and stepped out of the barrack. We knew he was going to look for the crowbar and ran after him, but he had already vanished in the dark.

We waited. An hour or so later, we heard his weak voice coming from somewhere. Bogembai was calling for me. I jumped up and ran to meet him. Bogembai was holding the crowbar; he was dirty and wet and was crawling slowly toward me. I could smell a sickly sweet odor and realized he was badly wounded.

The others came up, and we lifted Bogembai and carried him inside. We warmed up some water, rinsed and bandaged his wounds. Bogembai was unconscious; he had lost a lot of blood from a puncture wound on his thigh. He must have been stabbed with a dagger or a saber.

When he came to, I asked him what had happened. He struggled for air and sighed, "Yeseke, what's the point of talking about that? Everyone pushes us around."

I understood that it was one of our own drunk officers or soldiers who wounded him. Whenever the soldiers saw us support folks, they would rush at us with their fists; they tried to degrade us in any way possible. That must have been what happened with Bogembai as well.

We stayed at his bed the whole night, chanted a requiem, and waited for him to regain consciousness, at least for a minute, so he could say his good-byes. Bogembai died at dawn without ever waking up.

When the envoy came, not a single man moved. Mikhail had brought an officer with him. The officer said angrily, "Come on, bastards, who cares? What's one more or one less?" With that, he grabbed the guy closest to him and tried to push him through the door, but the guy pushed him off.

The officer said something to the Mikhail, who then said. "Come on, guys. Enough of your stubbornness. Provoking the officer will only cause trouble."

Then they both stepped out. We remained standing. We knew not to expect anything good from them. The death of an Asian man meant nothing to a Russian officer. What could one death mean in a war where blood was spilled every minute.

Suddenly, Mikhail ran back in, breathless, and said, "Guys, Alikhan Torey is coming to see you."

We cheered up. We had heard that on behalf of the tsar's administration, our fellow countryman Alikhan had come to the front. We had all hoped to meet him and talk to him. Our luck had turned around, and we would see him soon.

He entered in the company of two Russian officers. Even though we had never seen him before, we knew right away that it was Alikhan Torey.

Mikhail wanted to introduce him to us, but Alikhan Torey gestured him to stop and started the conversation himself, "How are you doing, fellow countrymen? I only now got a chance to meet you and talk to you. I hear you have a casualty among you. May he rest in peace. What was his name?"

"Sir, his name was Bogembai. If it's possible, we would like to bury him according to our customs," I said.

"So be it. Bury him today. I will come to his funeral too. Does someone among you know the Qur'an? We need to give absolution to the deceased."

We had such a person among us, and after lunch, Bogembai's grave was topped with a small hill. We knew that the grave would most likely disappear, but there was nothing we could do about that. We could not take him home. Alikhan Torey was with us at the funeral and even said a prayer.

When we came back to the barrack, there was food on the table. Alikhan Torey had ordered a ram butchered for the memorial. We chanted a requiem, commemorated the deceased, and over the memorial dinner, the Torey told us that the war would be over soon, and we would all go home. While the Torey spoke, the wretched Kasengazy was shoveling food in. His face glistened with grease, and he winked at me, "You should eat some cabbage. It's very good for you; it can cure all diseases." Not long after that we came home.

By an unfortunate quirk of fate, the honorable bogatyr, Bogembai, had been left behind in the Belarus ground, but the worthless Kasengazy had returned home unharmed. When saying his good-byes to me, Sabyr, from Beskargay, had wiped away a tear and asked, "Why do good people have such short lives?" I did not reply then. Later, Alikhan Torey was arrested and declared an enemy of the people.

"But I always remember how, in those hard days outside of Minsk, Alikhan squatted and read *ayat* (verses) from the Qur'an." My grandpa finished his story and read a prayer, like he always did when he commemorated Alikhan and his old friends. We said amen after Grandpa and crossed our hands over our faces.

Reflections

Grandpa Yesim was a great storyteller.

Soviet propaganda poster of the 'Dekulakization' Campaign: "Down with Wealthy Peasants in the Agricultural Villages." (Image from Wikipedia, "Dekulakization.")

In the evenings, when neighbors or guests gathered in the house, Grandpa Yesim would tell stories. He knew the Arabian Nights' tales by heart, and he was amazing at narrating them. He also made us read Treasure Island out loud, which had just been translated into Kazakh. I remember my grandpa retelling it later.

When the 'Dekulakization' ('Away with Wealthy Peasants') campaign started, Grandpa Yesim and his brother Alim were arrested as enemies of the people and taken to Pavlodar, where they were imprisoned for a few months. By a lucky chance, they stayed alive. Grandpa Yesim would sometimes say that it was thanks to Alim's curative skills; otherwise, they would have been in the land of the dead long ago.

Grandpa Yesim's Story

The twilight would die into dark, the door would creak, and the nightmare would begin. The wardens at the door would turn their noses away from the foul air and call out a name of a prisoner. A minute later, their next victim would cross the threshold of the ward. We did not know where they took him, but we guessed that he would not return.

After a while we would all start chanting a requiem. It became a habit with us.

I had been in that stinking ward for three months already. Once a week, one of us would be taken out of the ward. He would never come back. My brother and I tried not to think of what was coming to us, but a blunt fear slowly crept into our hearts. Someday the ward would show up at the door and call out my brother's name, or mine. Only the Lord knew who would be first.

A man could get used to anything, and my dearest wish was that my brother and I would stay in that ward as long as possible. I hoped that, God willing, the times would change and we would be set free. That was what I thought, and I had no better place on earth than that shabby room with my younger brother next to me.

Days were followed by nights. Several unlucky souls disappeared behind the squeaky door, never to return. We chanted the usual requiem, saying good-bye to the departed in our thoughts. We pitied them, but everyone thought of his own inevitable fate. Eventually, it was our turn. One evening the ward did not stop at the door. He paced quickly into the middle of the ward, stopped, and said, "Sapinov Alim, to the exit."

Everything went dark. I had asked God so many times for only one mercy: if we were not destined to live, I wanted to be taken away first.

My poor brother hunched over and shuffled off to the exit. I darted from my spot, caught up with him, and tried to put a bundle of clothes into his hands.

"Don't," Alim pushed away the bundle. He looked at me as if he was trying to give me some sign, but I didn't understand.

After Alim had left, the ward, as always, grew silent. Everyone was saying a requiem. Alone, I stood petrified at the door. I could not believe that I would never see my brother again.

"How could this happen?" I thought. For some reason, I had not sensed this impending disaster. Last night I had dreamed of our Malybay Lake, and when I woke up, I told my brother that we would be free soon; we would go home.

"Inshallah (God willing), Yesim. Whatever fate has in store for us, that is what we will get. Everyone has to drain his cup to the dregs," Alim said, but his face lit up and his eyes twinkled. He told me that he had dreamed of Malybay Lake last night too, and he knew that they would let us out soon.

That night I was alone, and I thought about my brother. I still felt certain that we would see each other soon.

We did indeed. At dawn the door squeaked quietly. Everyone was greatly surprised to see Alim alive and unharmed. Alim smiled and, without saying a word, he sat down and, as always, fell dead asleep immediately.

I could do nothing else but snuggle up to him, whispering words of prayer.

The next evening, Alim was ordered to come out again. No one said a requiem this time, and Alim returned later that evening. This continued for a whole week.

Finally, Alim was not called anymore, and people in the ward cheered up. Soon Alim was set free. As he was saying good-by to me, he whispered, "Yesim, you will get out soon, too. May God look after you." That was the first time I saw tears in the eyes of my younger brother, who was always reserved and stern.

After five more months in prison, I was also released to go home to my family. I cannot hold back my tears when I remember the day that I finally hugged my children and my family after such a long separation. After we all calmed down, and our lives got back to normal, I asked Alim to tell me what had happened to him.

This is what he told me.

Alim's Story

You know that Muslim Tatar guard who questioned us. He was pale, not a drop of blood in his face. They say that when murderers and torturers kill innocent people, their souls become an empty hole in their heart. That is why they are often very cowardly. Any cowardice creates cruelty. Our warden was one of those murderers and torturers. The more he tormented us, the more cowardly he became.

You remember that night. I was taken to an interrogation room where the warden was waiting. He suddenly rushed over to where I sat, held his revolver against my forehead, and yelled that he would kill me.

I told him, "My life is in God's hands, not yours."

As soon as I uttered those words, he spat curses and obscenities and punched me in the face with all his strength. I fell to the floor, and blood poured out of my nose. I lost consciousness. When I woke up, my eyes met his. He leaned over, placing his foot on my chest, and scrutinized my face. After a full minute, he could no longer hold my stare, and he turned away. Then he dampened a towel and said, "Sorry, old man. Here, wipe your face." He threw me the towel. I wiped the blood off my face and sat back down on the chair. The warden was quietly writing something on paper.

"Son..." I said. I still do not know if it was me talking or someone else using my voice.

"Son," I repeated, "you have a sick person at home."

"You bastard, what is that to you?" he almost flared up again.

You saw how he took me out of the ward again later. In the dead of night an attendant brought me back to the interrogation room. That same man was sitting there. He got up and said, "Aqsaqal, I am going to tell you something; you just listen."

The Warden's Story

Before the revolution, I studied literacy in a madrasa. My mother was a devout woman. My father lived on trade and was hardly ever at home. We lived well. But then the Red forces came, and the world split in half.

Through his Russian trader friend, my father got me placed in a mounted squadron with the Red Guards. My mother told me that, in a dream, she saw my father say that the saint-prophet Khidr[9] was helping the Red forces, and the Bolshevik Red Army would defeat the anti-Bolshevik White Army. She was the one who had advised my father to send me into a Red Guards squadron.

---

[9] EN: 'Khidr' is a legendary 'savior' figure in Muslim tradition. See esp. Paul Smith, *Khidr in Sufi Poetry: A Selection* (CreateSpace, 2012).

I was appointed squadron commander for my military merits in fighting the White (Tsarist) Army and Alash Orda (provisional Kazakh government) forces.

Later, when I was married and working in the State Political Directorate, we received an anonymous letter about some charismatic Muslim *hadrat*[10] who held gatherings in his house and was thought to be an anti-Soviet agitator. I was ordered to arrest him, or kill him if he resisted.

It was an order. If I tried to avoid it, I could lose my own head. I had arrested people before, but I had never had to face a religious minister, especially a *hadrat*.

I started to get ready for the trip, but then my wife said, "Khamidolla, I would rather you did not go anywhere." I asked her why. She pointed at her belly.

She knew what kind of job I had, but when she heard that I had to arrest a *hadrat*, she started begging me not to do it. "Don't darken your soul with that sin; don't anger God. We are expecting a baby, at least take pity on the baby. We will be cursed," she cried.

But what Union State Political Department officer would listen to his wife? That evening, I took two soldiers to assist me and went off to do my task.

I expected to see an old, crooked man, but instead I saw a strong, vital old man in front of me.

I screamed at him, "What are you thinking, old man, going against the Soviet government? I will show you how to slander Bolsheviks!"

The *hadrat* replied, "Son, we are all in the hands of God. If I am destined to die, that is the will of the Almighty. However, I am not against your government. I live on my own and serve God. I stay away from your politics."

I knew that if I did not stop him, the old man might stir up ideas in our heads.

So I arrested him, and we brought him out of his village.

---

[10] EN: 'Hadrat' is from Arabic and applied to respected social leaders who are religiously devout.

We came across a *mazar* (mausoleum) on our way, and the old man said, "Son, you are a Muslim too. Let me pray on the grave of our ancestors one last time."

I got angry, and swinging my whip, I pushed the old man in the back, forcing him to move on without any delays. The old man did not utter a word but headed for the graves.

I still do not understand what came over me then. Blind with rage, I pulled out my revolver and shot the old man twice, without aiming. One of the envoys jumped off his horse saying, "What a pity." He ran to the *hadrat* and lifted him up. The old man was whispering a prayer, and in a minute, he was dead. People from the village had heard the shots and were running over. The envoys said, "Chief, it's dangerous to stay here. Let's go."

On the way, we decided to say that the old man was shot trying to escape.

We arrived back late, so I didn't get home until morning.

Sad news was waiting for me: as soon as I had left, my wife went into labor and gave birth to a dead baby. Even though my wife never said so, I felt that she thought it was my fault. She kept on insisting that I should quit my job. How could she know that a KGB serviceman could not just quit.

After a while, my wife was pregnant again. She gave birth to a baby girl. She is already eleven, but the poor thing suffers so much. At night she gets seizures and we have to watch over her.

One day I mentioned to my wife that we had a healer in our prison. As soon as she heard about you, she started begging me to bring you to our home. Then during the questioning, you said that I had a sick person at home. When you looked at me, it seemed like it was the dead *hadrat* looking at me. Now that I think about it, if that *hadrat* had looked me straight in the eyes, I could not have shot him.

"That is my truth, Aqsaqal. Forgive me if you can. I don't think anyone can punish me more than I punish myself. If my daughter gets better, I will release you and your brother, and I will quit the police force. My departed mother said there was no sin that God would not forgive. If God is willing, I will devote the rest of my life to him."

Alim's Story (continued)

The warden's wife turned out to be a pleasant, kindhearted, and sweet woman. She offered me tea, but I refused and asked to see the ailing daughter.

When I looked at the girl, I knew she had the falling sickness. Life in prison had made me weak, so when I started treating her, I could hardly stay on my feet from fatigue. By the time I felt the girl was getting better, I was covered in sweat. I put the girl in bed and warned the parents to keep an eye on her.

I stepped into another room and washed my face. Then the hostess brought me some food. I ate a piece of meat and rinsed it down with some broth. Then I said a prayer and got up. The warden could do nothing but follow me.

That repeated for several days. On the sixth day, the girl recovered from her sickness; she became lively, happy, and agile. I said good-bye to the hostess and went back to prison.

Soon the warden called me and told me that I was free. I asked him to release my older brother instead of me.

"I can't do that," said the governor, "but my wife would take my daughter and leave me if I didn't release you at once. I promise your brother will be free in three or four months."

With that, we parted.

Grandpa Yesim's Story (continued)

When Alim was released, he went back to his old life. He treated people, charmed illnesses away, and carried out mullah (Islamic religious clerical) duties. He kept to himself and began to avoid people. He read books for days on end and became almost an ascetic.

As for me, I did not want to think about devoutness. On the contrary, I tried to be involved with people; I was eager for any conversations and stories.

District and regional officials often visited my home. Occasionally, I asked the headman about Khamidolla, who used to be the warden. He told me, "That dog Khamidolla got right under my skin. He had his Party membership card, but we found out he was attending a mosque, so we shot him. His woman was put into a loony bin."

I imagined the little daughter of Khamidolla, who was the reason why my brother and I escaped death. Where was she now? I decided not to tell Alim anything.

Reflections

So many human lives were ruined, mutilated; so many souls disappeared in the giant millstone of the Soviet regime, when the mask of justice covered cruelty and violence. It was a time when men were afraid, not of God, but of a man in a leather jacket with a Mauser rifle in his hands. Little gods of the new power set their rules everywhere, eradicating the free spirits from everyone and everywhere. People lived in hell while dreaming of a heavenly life for their children. Then all the slogans and invocations collapsed in an instant. The giant colossus on clay feet fell apart.

By that time the people dear to me were gone. Alim and Grandpa Yesim. But I remember how Grandpa Yesim would put me on his lap and say, "Do not trust this government. It won't last long. Work, do what you are told, but save your soul for better times."

I did not like Grandpa's words, but to my displeasure, he repeated them often. "What can I expect from an illiterate and uneducated man?" I thought then.

Little did I know that his was the last generation of strong-willed people who possessed genuine knowledge. They remained true to their principles and did not absorb the legacy of the Grand Chief.

I would put on my red Pioneer tie and sing songs about Lenin at the top of my voice.

Grandpa would listen, sigh, and with his voice filled with sadness, say, "Good boy, grandson, good boy!"

My father's older brother, Sattar, was declared an enemy of the people and thrown into prison. Much later, a man who had shared a prison cell with him visited us. He told us about the last days of Sattar, how he died. I wrote his story in my notebook.

The Cellmate's Story

It had been two days since the wardens made sure that Sattar would not survive. They had dragged his unconscious body across the place and had thrown him into the cell.

He had not had any food or water for two days already, but

severe pain quieted his hunger and thirst. Only his mind remained clear; thoughts crowded into his mind, one after another. Sattar knew that he was not going to leave that place alive. He knew his last hour was near, and there would be no one to close his eyes and say a prayer. In his thoughts he turned to God, repeating prayers he knew and asking the Almighty to forgive him his earthly sins.

One day had passed, and another was coming to its end. Sattar's soul was not in a hurry to leave his tormented body.

He suddenly remembered that old people said, if a man was having a hard time parting with his life, it meant that God did not absolve him of the sins he had committed on earth. Sattar tried to remember his sins. "Who needs me to stay here? Sin, sin, what is my sin?"

But no matter how hard he tried, nothing came to mind. "Maybe he did not have any sins, unless you could consider coming into this world a sin? No, that was God's will."

"Perhaps then, all sins are a function of the Creator's will? No. How could such a thought have occurred to me? God created man for good; all sins come from the evil one, from Satan. That is clear. Do I have sins before God? I must be sinful, just like everyone else on earth."

There had to be a sin. Sattar closed his eyes and tried to remember. His memory obligingly showed him pictures of his childhood. He tried to find some abominable behavior. Perhaps he hit someone, swore at someone, or offended someone when he was a boy? All his attempts were in vain. The dying man could not remember a single sin from his childhood. Hold on. What about… When Sattar remembered a particular event from long ago, his cheeks flushed.

He was in his home village, during the last years of the war; all that were left were elders, children, young girls, and the cripples who had returned from the war.

Teenagers like Sattar worked together on the thrashing floor from dawn until late at night. Every village also had a do-nothing, an idler like Koyken, who was Sattar's age.

One day, Koyken pulled Sattar aside conspiratorially. "Listen," he said haughtily. "This is what it means to become a man. Like other men, I sleep with women. It's fun." He burst into laughter when he saw Sattar's face redden.

As Sattar tried to leave, Koyken grabbed his hands, "Hey, snot, I haven't told you everything yet. Soon enough you can start doing it too."

"Keep your mouth shut, Koyken," Sattar snapped, walking away.

Koyken caught up with him and said that he had just eavesdropped on a conversation between Zhannat and Almy, two young women who worked on the thrashing floor. They were inseparable friends, and that good-for-nothing Koyken had been with one of them. He had overheard Zhannat say she was going to persuade me to sleep with her. So, of course, he had hurried over to deliver the news.

At dinner that evening, Koyken's words started to come true. Zhannat lavished attention on Sattar and did not leave his side, not even for a minute. As if by accident, she would touch his hair or push her plate closer to his.

At first, Sattar thought she was just taking care of him as a *zhenge* (the wife of an older brother or a close relative) would; her husband was Sattar's relative, after all. Even so, he tried to stay away from her.

In bed that night, though, the feel of warm breath against his skin woke him up. Someone was hugging him tight. Sattar wanted to scream, but a hot palm covered his mouth.

"Sattar, my sunshine, be quiet. It's me, Zhannat. Let's have some fun…but don't you dare to tell anyone. There we go, sweetie, there we go." She rolled onto her back and pulled Sattar with her.

Sattar jumped up and bolted off. Zhannat tried to catch him, but he had already disappeared.

Sattar saw his nocturnal visitor the next morning, but he hardly recognized her—her eyes were swollen, her face was pale. She must have cried the whole night.

The next day, Zhannat was transferred from the thrashing floor to another job.

Sattar went back to rummaging through his memories, trying to find his sinful deeds. But no, there was nothing that he could call a sin. He never took part in fights; occasionally he would get beaten up, but he never tried to fight back.

Suddenly, Sattar had an overpowering and painful desire to be sinful. Why hadn't he understood this sooner? It is easier for a sinner to part with this world. It was much scarier to leave this life when you were innocent, like a child. All at once, he wanted to commit at least one sin. He felt some spring uncoil inside of him, some wild power grow.

Now he was thinking of his zhenge Zhannat with regret. If he had sinned then, he would not be in this cold barrack now. Koyken, who was up to his ears in sin, was living the good life as a foreman in the kolkhoz. "What was the point of not committing a single sin in my life? I am leaving this earthly realm anyway, innocent and free of sin. I have to try to get up; maybe then I'll be able to sin." But his body seemed to have turned into stone; only his right arm showed any sign of life.

Sattar thought of his home village again, and of Ayna. Where was she now? "I'll wait," she had whispered when they parted. "Wait for me, sweetheart."

The sound of a door opening interrupted Sattar's thoughts. A mustached guard leaned over Sattar and stared into the prisoner's face. "Godspeed," the Father used to say on such occasions.

"Godspeed," Sattar said to himself as he decided to rip out the warden's mustache and make that his sin. He lifted his right arm, but it shook and fell back down before reaching the face of his torturer. "Such a pity, what can I do now?" He tried to kick the guard, but he couldn't move his leg.

Then it dawned on him—pulling out the guard's mustache would not be enough. It was not really a sin. Taking revenge on a villain like him was a good deed. This scum used his power to beat and kill innocent people. No, to make it count as a sin, he would have to beat an innocent and pure person.

Sattar's mind became muddled, sinking in and out of darkness. But one thought kept fluttering through his brain: he had to commit a sin, no matter what. Then he thought, "Would it be enough of a sin to think ill of a decent and pure person?" Even for that he would need some strength, and he had none. It would be a considerable sin to slander a man, even if it was just in his thoughts.

Humans seemed to have a limitless ability for making false allegations, for backstabbing, degrading, or insulting others, especially inside a prison. Sometimes the guards would urinate into the soup, laughing, and then give the soup to the poor prisoners to eat. Beating or killing was a common activity for the guards.

Sattar suffered through beatings many times, but he did not blame anyone. It seemed to him that someone upstairs had spread a bad disease, and everyone had gone mad with it. Grandpa said that the time would come when a son would become his father's enemy, and mothers and daughters would become foes. Sattar had been destined to live in that time. This was it.

But not everyone had lost reason. Other prisoners seemed to be in their right mind still, but their lives were worse than a dog's.

The mustached guard came back, this time with his partner. "There's another one done," he pointed at Sattar. "Put him on the sled; we'll bury him."

The partner approached Sattar and said, "Well, would you look at that? I think he's still alive. This enemy seed turned out to be tough. He hasn't even had water for two days."

"That's all right; take him anyway. If he isn't dead yet, he'll croak on the way."

The partner did not say anything. It happened often. Sometimes they would bury someone who was still moaning.

The two of them picked up Sattar and threw him onto the pile of dead bodies.

Sattar fell on top of a dead woman. He remembered Ayna, that pure, innocent soul. "That is who I will think ill of." He tried to compare her with Zhannat, but then felt sorry for doing so. With the last drop of his strength he cried, "Ayna."

The guard heard that barely audible groan and slammed a shovel onto Sattar's head.

His mind went dark; the light dimmed and faded away.

The sled, loaded with dead bodies, glided slowly toward the forest.

Reflections

One of the victims who suffered from Socialism was my mother, Bizhamal.

There were six of us in the family. We were half-starved and half-naked. Life was very hard. Mother worked in the kolkhoz her entire life, but was left without a pension. In spite of everything, she tried to teach us and did all she could to make sure we got an education.

Dinnertime would bring conversations. My mother, pleased with her life, would say, "The happy enjoy even plain water as food."

She often recalled how difficult it was for her to raise us. Her most fervent prayer was for no more wars. She had to live through the frightful times when the village would be seized by either Red or White (Tsarist) forces. They had to hide from both. Her memory held many stories from those dark years.

She often told us about one incident that she had witnessed. To be honest, I did not like that story. "What could she know?" I thought to myself. "She is not class-conscious. She can't read. What could she understand about class struggle?"

At school we would sing songs about our valiant Red Army: "We are the Red Horsemen." We wanted to be like the Soviet general Semyon Budyonny and the legendary division commander Kliment Voroshilov, who were our childhood idols. My mother's story was somehow strangely out of tune with my idea of the Red Army; it brought discord and doubt into my young heart. I could not hide the discomfort her stories caused me.

My mother had an older brother named Kabiden. He was unusually tall for his age, a skinny fifteen-year-old boy with a sweet, shy nature. If he happened to talk about himself, his cheeks would blush crimson with embarrassment. Whenever my mother talked about him, she would give a heavy sigh and wander off into her thoughts for a while.

My Mother's Story

It happened in the 1920s, when the Red and White forces were taking turns seizing power in the village. Whoever came, the village would welcome them and treat them as dear guests. But after they had eaten and rested, they would make passes at the young girls and women. So the girls and women would hide in the forest before anyone arrived, sneaking back home at night for some food. Only the elders and the children stayed at home.

One time, the Red forces showed up in the village. There were so many of them, it seemed they flooded the whole world. People in the village kept their heads down, as if sensing trouble. The Reds were mainly Russian, though occasionally you could see some Tatars and Kazakhs among them.

An officer in a leather jacket strapped with ammo belts said something to a Kazakh soldier, and the soldier shouted at Kabiden, "Hey, kid, go get some water for the horses, and hurry up!"

Kabiden was accustomed to watering horses. He took equal care of both the Reds' and the Whites' horses. This time, though, there were so many horses, he could not cope with all of them by himself.

He deftly pulled one bucket after another out of the well, quickly pouring the water into the watering trough, but no matter how hard he tried, there was not enough water. One of the men lost patience with him and yelled, "Come on, kalbit (an extremely offensive nickname for people from Central Asia) hurry up!" hitting him twice with a whip. Kabiden reeled, leaned on the well stand, stood up for a bit, and then seemed to lose his strength and dropped to the ground.

The officer in the leather jacket gathered all the village people together and started asking questions through an interpreter.

"When the Whites come here, who helps them? Did the Basmachi[11] come? Do they have any relatives here?"

People were scared to death by the belligerent air of the man and tried to cajole him. Some very talkative brownnosers bent over backward trying to show the officer how helpful they were.

The village people had had enough of the Whites too, but how could they tell the Reds that? Who could promise that the Whites would not replace the Reds again? There would be another interrogator then, asking the same questions, but about the Reds.

The best thing was to stay quiet, as if we did not know anything and had not heard anything.

The officer was not content with the evasive replies. He pulled his saber out of its sheath and put it over old Turamys's head. The old man shook with fear and pointed at Kabiden, lying unconscious by the well, "That one watered their horses."

The officer nodded, and immediately two Red Army soldiers grabbed Kabiden under his arms, poured a bucket of water over his head, and dragged him over to the officer.

---

[11] EN: 'The Basmachi' were a Central Asian Muslim military movement who resisted the Bolsheviks from 1918 down to the early 1930s. See esp. Fazal-ur-Rahim Khan Marwat, *The Basmachi Movement in Soviet Central Asia: A Study in Political Development* (Emjay Books International, 1985). It is known in Central Asian scholarship as the Turkestan Liberation Movement. See esp. A. Ahat Andican, *Turkestan Struggle Abroad: From Jadidism to Independence* (Haarlem, Netherlands: SOTA, 2007).

"Did you water Whites' horses?" asked the interpreter, pointing at Turamys. Kabiden did not say anything, but as usual, his cheeks turned red.

"I see. We'll take them with us; we'll have another talk," said the officer saddling his horse.

The Red Army left the village and took the old man and the young kid with them. The next morning, the villagers went looking for Turamys and Kabiden and found their chopped bodies hanging on trees in a small forest.

People gathered the unfortunate victims' body parts, which were hanging all over the branches, and committed them to the ground.

Years passed. My mother died. She never changed her attitude toward the Reds and often mentioned her older brother in her prayers.

But we kept on singing the song we had grown to like so much.

Reflections

Another who suffered from the Soviets was my father Kabdyzhappar. In 1938 he was drafted by the army. In 1939 he fought against the White Finns. Then the Great Patriotic War (World War II) started. Father did not return home until 1943, and he had lost an eye in the war. Although handicapped, he worked in a state farm until 1967, with no vacations or days off. That was

Kazakh Soviet propaganda poster from the Great Patriotic War (1939-45) representing the recent forced conversion to Cyrillic script (1940), which followed a forced conversion from the original Arabic to the 'internatinal' Latin script (1928-40). It reads: "Let's Give all the Metal We can for the Fatherland!" Courtesy of the A. Kasteev State Museum of Arts (Almaty, Kazakhstan).

the practice then: to pay money in place of vacations.

Father was a kind man with a generous and open heart. He had a very special respect for people.

He was lucky to have evaded Soviet ideology. Until the day he died, he prayed salat, *fasted, and remained a God-fearing and dedicated Muslim man.*

Father had to endure severe hardships. His life before the war was full of stories and adventures.

Here is one of the stories from his childhood.

My Father's Story

It was early in the morning, and everyone in the house was already up and getting ready for the road. As I understood it, Father had decided to move to Altay, away from kolkhoz activists.

They packed dishes, blankets, pillows, and clothes. Everyone was fussing about, tying up our simple belongings into bundles. I was the only one standing still, apart from the others.

It was scary. For some reason no one had talked to me about the move until today. When the packing was finished, we all sat down in a semicircle, and Grandpa said a prayer, blessing our travel.

Father got off his knees and headed for the exit. Women, who had been holding back their tears, started weeping. Men tried to console them, calm them down, but their sobs and sad sighs could be heard for a long time. It had to be hard for those poor souls to abandon everything they had earned and saved over the years.

It is not easy to leave your homeland, where you know every stone, and take off like a tumbleweed. What would be waiting for us there in that strange land? Who would be waiting for us there with open arms?

My mother, now departed, may she rest in peace, came up to me, tightened her arms around me, kissed me a few times then gave me a bundle and said in a firm voice, "Son, there was no other choice. Be careful and look after yourself." She wiped her tears and swiftly stepped away from me.

My world began to collapse. They were leaving me alone here among strangers. "No, I won't stay. No matter what, I will go with them," I decided.

Grandpa came up to me. "Son, be good. You will stay with relatives. You have to understand; it's safer for you here. You are still a kid; they won't touch you. It is hard for us. Try to understand." With those words, he got into the wagon, and the horses set off.

I was standing and staring at my father, who was trying hard to avoid my eyes, pretending to be very busy. I suddenly realized that Father had been acting strange lately, even weird. For the past two or three days, he had not let me out of his sight, not even for a minute.

When we stopped at the neighboring village, he whispered with Kospan, the shepherd, for a long time. Then he called me over and said, "Koseke, here he is for you. He is still young, but what can we do? He'll just have to make peace with his fate. I beg you to take care of him. Make him your helper; let him tend sheep."

Kospan hesitated, "Hell! I don't know. Times are hard now; I can't even stand up for myself all the time."

"I have no other choice, Koseke. I accept all your conditions," my father said. He got up, letting Kospan know the conversation was over.

The only thing I understood then was that my father wanted me to make some money. I was not upset at all. Kospan did not live far from us. "I will just run home," I thought, with boyish unconcern. Besides, Kospan was a relative and was well known for his open and kind nature. I also had heard from Grandpa that those who worked on the state farm could drink plenty of sheep's milk. "At least I won't be hungry," I mused about my future life.

My father and I left Kospan and, as we walked, Father repeatedly stopped to hug me or pet me. I was surprised at my father's unusual behavior, but I assumed he just felt bad that he was sending me to work when I was still too young.

"How hard could it be? Tending sheep is not that bad," he said.

I had not really thought that my family would abandon me, but now it was beginning to sink in. I was supposed to stay, but Father, Mother, Grandpa, all my brothers and sisters, my entire family were leaving me alone to the mercy of fate.

I stood stock-still. I was overwhelmed with a feeling of enormous unfairness. When the wagons set off, I let out a howl and charged after my family, screaming something, tears streaming down my face. When I reached the last wagon, my younger brother gave me his hand. I pulled with all my strength and jumped onto the wagon.

Father jumped off the first wagon and came over. He yanked me off the wagon and gave me a hard slap.

Everyone started yelling; someone even stood up for me. Then my father's sonorous voice made everyone quiet.

I was suffocating with tears. Paying no attention to my cheek, which was burning from the slap, I ran back to the wagon.

With his strong hand, Father pushed me away. I fell down and did not get up again. I lay in the dust and cried for a long time. When I finally got up, the wagons were all gone.

It was too late to catch up with them, so I picked up the bundle my mother had given me and shuffled back to the village, to the old Kospan.

Father and the rest came back two years later. Grandpa was not with them anymore. He had died in faraway lands. The rest had returned safely. My brothers and sisters had even started speaking Russian.

Many years later I asked my father, "Why did you leave me then? Why didn't you take me with you?"

Father let out a heavy sigh, "Son, when we set out on the road then, we did not think we would ever return. Mother could not get a job because in the eyes of the Soviet government I was a kulak, that is, a relatively affluent farmer. But food was scarce and we were beginning to starve, so Grandpa and I decided to leave for Altay. Only God knew what would happen there. It would be unfamiliar people, unfamiliar language, unfamiliar customs. That's why we decided to leave you here in your homeland. If we were bound to perish, at least you would stay alive and continue our name. Your younger brother was too small, but you could stand up for yourself and earn your bread."

Certainly, if my father had told me that back then, I probably would not have understood. For many years, I remembered that hard slap and how he had pushed me away. I saw it as cruelty and incredible unfairness. I did not know that my father's severity was necessary; it was because of his love and his wish to save his child from hardships. Now that I have become a father and a grandfather, I understand. When I watch my children and grandchildren, I often remember my own childhood, those distant years. I see the tracks of the wagon; I feel my cheeks ablaze, and I think that an elder's strictness and severity would not hurt them.

Reflections

The events I have mentioned deepened my doubts about the infallibility of Socialist guidelines. I cannot say it included everyone, but I developed a distrust of Communists, especially those in charge, because of their hypocrisy and duplicity. Their words did not match their actions. Our generation did not participate in the Great Patriotic War, but we, who are now in our sixties, saw veterans who returned from war and those who spent their childhoods in the starving times of the troubled years. Many of them are not alive anymore, but I want to look back on one of them. His name was Daulet.

Excursion

During Soviet times people lived tolerably well only when Leonid Brezhnev was in power (1962-84). Before him and after him people were tortured with slogans; they were pulled back and forth. We would often sit around the *dastarkhan* (the cloth spread on the floor for dinner) after Party meetings, and the now-deceased Daulet would remember his childhood and sigh heavily.

"There were six of us in the family, one smaller than the other."

That was how his stories usually began.

"To feed us kids, Mother took freight trains to Semey to sell some petty wares. We children would go to school, or even outside, in turns because we did not have enough clothing and shoes for everyone. I envied my older sister because she had tarpaulin boots with foot wraps, and I wished for the time when I could have some; then I could go out and play with our neighbor Sergey's kids.

"In the evenings, if our mother was late, my sister and I would exchange frightened glances. We were the oldest, so our mother would wake us up early, before she left, to whisper what we were supposed to do that day. The babies enjoyed their sweet sleep, and our mom closed the door quietly behind her.

"When things got worse, our mom would say, 'For the blissful, even water is soup.' Now I understand that she was trying to console herself, to get some strength. She didn't want to call down the wrath of God with excessive laments. It was wartime…"

Daulet always sadly added that special qualifier, "It was wartime."

There was also an associate professor who attended the meetings. He was much older, round and solid as a pool ball. His name was Kaiyr, and he had been the head of the propaganda department for the regional Party committee.

After Party committee meetings, everyone would go down to the cafeteria, which was stocked with vodka and cognac. The first secretaries of the regional committees would bring smoked meats and *kazy* (horse-meat sausage) with them. We, the authorized officials of the regional committee, would visit with them.

When Kaiyr spoke of his life during those hard times, he would describe his business trips to the districts, where they had been served handsomely, where they ate and drank to their heart's content. Then he would finish each story with a satisfied, "It was wartime."

At those words, I would look at Daulet out of the corner of my eye. Even though he would be purple with tension and anger, he would stay quiet, not showing how Kaiyr's words affected him.

Kaiyr, not suspecting any problem, would finish one story and move on to another, each as worthless and empty as the one before and each with the very same ending, "It was wartime."

"War is war no matter what war it is, isn't it?" I once asked my uncle, my father's brother, who had returned with awards and wounds.

"We fought for justice," he replied sharply.

But can a war be just?

Reflections

During Soviet times, the government began easing up on religious matters when Brezhnev came to power. Later, Mikhail Gorbachev also showed loyalty to religion. By the time my father retired, the elders asked him to become an imam in the district mosque. In those years, I was already distanced from old atheistic dogmas and beliefs; I slowly developed an interest in religion, an inclination for it. My father and I often stayed up all hours of the night talking about God. We had no heated discussions or misunderstandings as there was nothing to argue about; there was only a desire to understand and accept what had been in the heart for so long, but had been forcedly deafened. One day, Father told me a story about a bloody incident that occurred in the first years of Soviet power, during the Muslim holiday Eid al-Adha (Feast of Sacrifice).

My Father's Story

I had read about the Red and White forces in books; I had watched movies about them, so I had heard of them. But I only heard about the Basmachi, or *Karalar* (the Blacks) as people would call them, from the elders in our village. As a storyteller, I am certainly not fit to even shine the shoes of our villages's aqsaqals, but I will try to relay what I remember.

It was the time when Soviet power was just getting started. Agricultural cooperatives were setting up everywhere, but there were more people holding weapons in their hands than there were holding shovels. Folks in the village had just come to terms with the Soviets when the Whites barged in, retreating from the Reds. Soviet sympathizers were lined up and shot; their houses were burned. Like an avalanche, the Whites attacked defenseless people, destroying everything in their way. Then they disappeared into China, as the elders say.

Before people had time to come to their senses, the Reds arrived and started propagating Soviet power among the people. A red flag fluttered on top of the village council building once again. Those who had betrayed local activists to the Whites were brought to the square, lined up, and shot by the Reds.

"A dog's death for a dog," said one elder. "It was too bad for the children; the poor things were left alone," other elders sympathized.

As soon as the wounds had healed and the people had settled back into peaceful lives, armed horsemen showed up again. These were the ones people called "Karalar."

None of the elders could really explain the reason for that name. Perhaps they knew who the Karalar were and why they took to arms, but they kept quiet. However, they freely admitted that, when Soviets first began to take power, many people did not agree with the changes and tried to resist as much as they could.

I looked at them cautiously, surprised that they dared to say such things.

Once I had mentioned in class that the Blacks had had a leader, a true hero named Zhaiylkhan.

My history teacher had grown immediately angry and had yelled, "He was a bandit, a *Basmachi!*" The next day, he had called my parents to the school.

Only my older brother, who worked in the district center, had been able to put out that fire.

So those Blacks, the Basmachi, had not joined the Whites or the Reds. When they arrived in the village, they were few in number. Their leader was Zhaiylkhan. They especially hated the village activists, for whom they had no mercy.

Daiyrbay, who had just been appointed police chief, was frustrated. For a month now, he and ten policemen had been following Basmachi gangs, trying to locate Zhaiylkhan, but they had had no luck.

Zhaiylkhan had his people in every village, and he knew the local land like the back of his hand. He was playing with the inexperienced Daiyrbay like a cat playing with a mouse, sometimes even sneering at him. So it was not so much Daiyrbay following the Basmachi as it was the Basmachi watching Daiyrbay. Though they never engaged in open combat, the Blacks had killed a few policemen in accidental shootings.

As he returned to the district center, tired and worn out, Daiyrbay knew that he would not be able to catch the gang by himself.

He and Zhaiylkhan had actually grown up together in the same village. Daiyrbay remembered him as rowdy and liking to fight, having no mercy for anyone.

"I'll catch you one of these days," Daiyrbay muttered, gritting his teeth as he thought about the many unsuccessful nights following the Black gangs.

He had to think of something. Maybe he could arrest everyone who knew Zhaiylkhan, starting with his younger brother, Rakhymkhan. Rakhymkhan was an activist, a member of an agricultural cooperative. When Daiyrbay remembered him, his stomach churned. When they were kids, Rakhymkhan would often smack Daiyrbay around, and perhaps since then, Daiyrbay had been afraid of him. He wished he could send Rakhymkhan somewhere far away. In due time, he would be able to do that. He thought of the two dead policemen. Yes, Zhaiylkhan had shot one of them, so Rakhymkhan could be brought in for that. Daiyrbay smiled; payback was near, and for both brothers at the same time.

Rakhymkhan knew immediately the reason for the summons. He stood before Daiyrbay and said sternly, "You called; I came. What do you want, 'Chief' Daiyrbay?"

"Rakha, we're on the same side here. I wanted to ask your advice," Daiyrbay said, pretending not to hear the sarcasm in Rakhymkhan's voice.

"I wish I would never have to see you or my bandit brother," Rakhymkhan continued in the same tone. "The blood of innocent people is on your hands, both of you. You two are responsible for the tears of their mothers and children. The only difference is that you're a public officer, and my brother is a bandit, but you both share the same guilt. What do you want?"

Angrily, Daiyrbay jumped up and grabbed his revolver. Rakhymkhan did not bat an eye.

Daiyrbay calmed himself; he needed Rakhymkhan's help. "Brother, let us forget old grudges; this isn't the time to settle scores. You have a chance to prove your loyalty to the Soviets. You know where your brother is hiding; tell him to surrender voluntarily, or more blood will flow."

Rakhymkhan was silent. Daiyrbay was right; each day Zhaiylkhan acquired more sins. The government had long arms; it would be better for him to surrender to it—the sooner, the better.

"I do know where he is hiding," Rakhymkhan took a deep breath.

"If you know, then take me there. You only need to show me where; I will do the talking."

"All right, let's say I take you to him. Will Zhaiylkhan give up, just like that? His people watch your every step. He could kill you instead."

"Yes…" Daiyrbay said slowly, unsure what to do. Silence fell over the room.

Rakhymkhan broke the quiet.

"There is only one way out."

"Come on, Rakha, just tell me where he is. You don't even have to come with us; we can do it without you," Daiyrbay said.

"He will certainly come home for Eid al-Adha (the Muslim Feast of Sacrifice). He always observes the holiday by coming home to pray to his ancestors," Rakhymkhan said, as though he and his brother had different ancestors.

Daiyrbay paused to think, suddenly suspicious. Why would Rakhymkhan, who had bristled at the first mention of his brother, suddenly become so cooperative? Could it be a trap? Rakhymkhan was Zhaiylkhan's brother. Daiyrbay thought of wolves; they always killed their weak or wounded fellows. Perhaps, Rakhymkhan understood that Zhaiylkhan was nearing his end and had decided to finish him off?

Thoughts flooded Daiyrbay's mind and made it roar. It happened to him every time. As soon as he had to think of something serious, he head filled with noise. He thought of how solid Rakhymkhan's fists were. It occurred to him, "What if Rakhymkhan was a spy?" He grew tired of speculating, so he gave up, making a decision, "All right, I'll deal with Rakhymkhan later. For now, I'll focus on getting his brother."

Beads of sweat covered Rakhymkhan's brow. At any cost, he had to persuade his brother to give up. Enough blood had been shed. Besides, if he did not help the police now, Daiyrbay would find a way to get revenge.

"How had someone like Daiyrbay been given power? That coward had never been able to stand up to the brothers before. He must be elated at this turn of events."

It was all because of his brother. He thought of their mother's face. "Poor mother, you could not have imagined that your two sons would become enemies." Yes, his brother was his enemy. From the very start, Zhaiylkhan had taken issue with public authorities, had gotten into arguments. He had grabbed a rifle and become a Basmachi. His gang was about thirty strong, half of them Russian.

"I will help you catch my brother, Daiyrbay. There's no other way. I do understand; it's the class struggle. There can be no pity for family or friends."

"Rakha, I feel for you. It has to be hard to go against your own brother. But you're right; it is the class struggle, and it will be cruel."

"I have one request. Do not shoot my brother, Daiyrbay. Let him go to trial. He will not resist."

"I will try not to, Rakhymkhan, but you know your brother. If he sees me, I doubt he will hold his temper."

"Zhaiylkhan will surrender on his own; I guarantee it. I will be with him, and I will not allow bloodshed."

"All right, Rakhimkhan, you've given me your word. I trust you."

"Daiyrbay, no one knows better than me how cowardly your little chicken heart is. I'm warning you; don't let your fear make mountains out of molehills. God only knows what your fear will make you see. Remember, my brother will be unarmed. Don't be scared. If you kill him—I will tear your throat out."

Daiyrbay colored with impotent rage and thought, "You dog. You're just like your brother, thinking about biting me. You will not get away with that. Just give me time; I'll get even with you."

But out loud he said, "What are you talking about, Rakha? If he is your brother, he is not a stranger to me. We are relatives after all. Calm down, I won't lay a finger on him."

It was only a few days until Eid al-Adha. They talked over the final details of the upcoming operation and parted.

Aisha heard the hoofbeats and, thinking it was her husband coming to Eid, ran outside to meet him. But instead of her husband, she saw her brother-in-law, Rakhymkhan, slowly getting off his horse, dark as the darkest storm cloud. Aisha was at a loss, trying to think of how to send a message to her husband, telling him not to come.

Rakhymkhan guessed Aisha's thoughts and said, "I came because I need to talk with my brother. Don't worry, I'm alone."

Zhaiylkhan arrived soon. Aisha was shaken up and told him, "Brother-in-law is waiting for you. His coming is a bad omen; I feel it. Maybe you should just leave now, while you're still alive."

"Oh, Aisha, if my brother has come for my soul in the days of the sacred Eid, there is nothing to be done. The family will all be here. It's a big holiday today; we need to celebrate and then what shall be, shall be."

Zhaiylkhan leaned his rifle against the wall, performed ablution, and went in to say a prayer. He had a few bowls of tea, tried some flatbread, and then turned to his brother, "How is your government, still in its place?"

Rakhymkhan was silent for a moment and then replied to Zhaiylkhan, "This government will stay for a long time. You need to lay down your weapons and surrender. It will mitigate your guilt."

"What guilt are you talking about? I wish for a different rule; you do not accept our rule. So you and I have the same guilt. We are equal in it."

"Your rule is an illusion; it never existed. You protect something that is not there."

"That's true. I don't know for sure what our rule should be, but I do know that your regime is crap. How are you deadbeats and illiterates going to govern the people?"

"Soviet government is the power of the poor. Remember that."

"Then what am I? Am I a millionaire? How come I turn out to be guilty? Tell me that. Why do we get exiled to Siberia, deprived of everything we earned through honest work?"

Rakhymkhan was about to reply when some horsemen suddenly arrived at the yurt.

"You traitor! How could you? And on Eid al-Adha!" Zhaiylkhan roared as he jumped up and ran for his rifle.

Rakhymkhan pulled out his revolver and yelled, "Zhaiylkhan! Don't move or I will shoot you. You're surrounded. Think about the children. If you resist, they will burn everyone." Then he fired a shot into the air.

Daiyrbay charged into the room at the signal, with his gun in his hand. He paid no attention to Rakhymkhan, who was pleading, "He surrendered on his own, with no resistance," and shot Zhaiylkhan twice point-blank. Rakhymkhan's blood rushed to his head and, in a craze, he rushed at Daiyrbay.

When the other policemen came in, Rakhymkhan was standing over Daiyrbay, his hands covered in blood, trying to shake something slimy off his fingers.

Daiyrbay, with his throat torn out, was writhing and wheezing on the floor.

One of the policemen slammed his fist into the side of Rakhymkhan's head; another shot him.

They say the souls of those who die during Eid al-Adha go straight to heaven. I do not know if heaven's gate was waiting for all three of these men, or only one of them. The old men preferred not to talk about it.

Reflections

Now, everyone knows that the stories about the hard life of the nation, about the many lives lost in the years of constructing Socialism, are all historical truth. There is no need to prove otherwise. The most important question is, were all those victims necessary? I think that future generations will attempt to come to terms with the atrocities, they will try to find an answer to that question. All the playing with Socialist ideas led to severe social turmoil. Those who come after us need to understand and recognize that.

CHAPTER 2
THE SPECTER THAT HAUNTED EUROPE

To understand how Socialism arose in Kazakhstan, one should turn to the implementation of the ideas of Karl Marx and Friedrich Engels. On February 21, 1848, their joint work, *The Communist Manifesto*, was published in German. It began with, "A specter is haunting Europe—the specter of communism."

A rational person may find these words frightening, to say the least. A specter is not a part of reality, and it has no chance of becoming real. Its goal is to remain a specter, and that is all. The idea of a specter itself is dangerous.

The *Manifesto* starts with those words and ends with the slogan, "Working men of all countries, unite!" The authors divided all of humankind into two mutually exclusive camps: the exploiters and the exploited, that is, the workers or 'proletariat'. This conflict could be resolved only if the exploiters, as a class, were eradicated and the dictatorship of the proletariat was established. Toward that end, workers throughout the world had to unite and start a worldwide revolution. At the beginning of the twentieth century, that fatal idea found Russian supporters, who put it into practice. People suffered through an unforeseen spiritual tragedy, a convulsion beyond comparison.

Karl Marx talked about a specter, an airy spirit that haunted Europe, but gradually that specter spread throughout the entire world. His idea was realized in Bolshevism, headed by Lenin. When analyzing materials related to that period, the conclusion is that Bolshevism, in essence, was a political and terrorist force. Populists and Socialists were in league with the terrorists; admittedly, they were such themselves. There is sufficient and substantial evidence to support this claim. It is also known that other criminal organizations joined the Bolsheviks. Bolshevism found support in the illiterate and ignorant masses of common people. That strategy led them to victory. Their widely propagated slogan, "Bolshevism is the gravedigger for (profiteering) exploiters," had staggering success.

The Agony of Socialism

Various Kazakh Soviet propaganda posters, a number using Latin script (1928-40). Courtesy of the A. Kasteev State Museum of Arts (Almaty,

When Karl Marx talked about the specter that haunted Europe, he only meant that the proletarian revolution would happen in several prepared and developed countries. Objectively, that was a utopian idea. If it had remained a utopia, there would have been no danger of Socialism. However, the situation changed with the rise of Russian Bolshevism and its chief, Lenin. He introduced amendments into Marx's theory, asserting that imperialism was the highest moribund level of capitalism. Therefore, a proletarian revolution was possible in any country, not only in developed countries, and it did not have to occur in several countries at the same time. A proletarian revolution was possible in a backward country, where capitalistic relations were only beginning to develop. If only Lenin's addition had remained merely a theoretical discourse. The October Revolution of 1917 celebrated the victory of the ideas of Marx and Lenin, the ideas of Communism. Because Kazakhstan, at that time, was a remote colony of Russia, the specter of Communism settled there as well.

The Socialist society was based on two foundations. The first was collective property; the second was godlessness.

In order to assert their rule, Communists began by changing the types of ownership. For that, they introduced forced collectivization. Those who opposed it and tried to defend their rights were dispossessed; their property was confiscated, and they were exiled, executed, or destroyed.

Propaganda for the new lifestyle grew stronger every day. People had to make sure that the old days would not come back.

However, the policy drew discontent and protests in Kazakhstan. People, with weapons in hand, tried to fight the new regime. In the 1930s, there was a wave of insurgency against Bolshevism. The Soviet government put it down with a heavy hand. The best representatives of the nation were killed and tortured as a result of such clashes. Those who survived, fled abroad, leaving their homeland. Those horrible pages of history were made public only after Bolshevism had been defeated and the country had gained its sovereignty.

I remember the tales of the elderly Beysen, who knew many stories related to that time. The elderly Beysen usually started with the words, "There were thirty of them . . ."

The Elderly Beysen's Story

Azel, the head of the State Political Directorate (SPD), was worried. He was flooded with orders and instructions from above, all concerning one thing: immediately finding everyone who resisted collectivization, who terrorized the poor, and then seizing and destroying them. "Strike and smash" was the only decree from the authorities. He would be glad to obey, but he was lacking the forces. Only ten soldiers were in his command. The common people accepted the resistance gangs, the Basmachi, which were usually made up of middle- and low-income peasants, though their leaders were the sons of wealthy peasants or herdsmen. Azel knew that he would not be pardoned if he failed. He had to think of something, and think fast, but he had no one to even consult with. It was no use trying to get help from those in charge.

He was sitting in agonizing contemplation in his office, when there was a knock at his door. The man who entered seemed familiar to Azel, but he could not remember where he might have seen him. Azel looked at him expectantly, but the visitor was quiet, hoping perhaps that Azel would remember him.

Finally, Azel lost patience and asked, "Who are you? What do you want?"

"Aze, don't you recognize me? I am Mikhail. How could you forget me? Come on, search your memory."

The chief squirmed. Wasn't Mikhail in Mongolia? What is this bastard doing here? There must be a reason why he has shown up now. I need to destroy him before he blabs something about that time when he was an informer for the governorate police, and the SPD hired him to track and kill one of the Kazakh nationalists.

"Aze, no need to be afraid," Mikhail said. "You can kill me anytime, but for now, I can be useful to you."

Azel thought about the Basmachi; maybe he could use Mikhail for that. Azel decided to share his concerns with Mikhail, but not to trust him.

"Why should I be afraid of you? I have the power, the weapons; your life is in my hands. No one would charge me with murder; everyone knows you are a bloodsucker."

"Aze, I do not fear death. Everyone has to die at some point. I came to help you…but not for free, of course."

"All right then. Tell me how you can help me."

"You have Basmachi gathered close by. They will not stop until they destroy you and your rule."

"Quit spouting nonsense. There is no force that can destroy our rule. They will fail. Just say what you have in mind."

"I came to tell you how to crush the bandits."

Azel paused to think. That was what he needed. Mikhail knew everything; he knew many ways to exterminate people. Yes, he would have to use Mikhail's services. As soon as Mikhail was done with his business, though, Azel would eliminate him.

"Aze, don't worry. I will only give you some advice and then disappear. You know, if you kill me, you will call down the wrath of God upon yourself," Mikhail said, as if reading Azel's mind.

Yes, the bastard was right. But if he were to flee abroad, it would be in secrecy; nobody need know that I had worked with him. I'll need to protect myself; for now, though, I will listen to this scoundrel.

With such thoughts, Azel looked at Mikhail, inviting him to continue the conversation.

"You need to destroy the bandits."

Azel nodded.

"To stop a fire, you create a counterfire so that, when everything burns down, the fire will stop on its own. Imagine that the bandits are a fire. To counter it..."

Azel jumped up, not listening to the rest of Mikhail's words. What an idiot I've been! Why hadn't I thought of that? I need to organize another gang to counter the existing one.

Azel looked at Mikhail, "I get it. You'll organize the gang; it's your idea after all."

"Aze, the Kazakhs have a saying, 'The wolf and the courageous man both find their food along the way.' Give me weapons and people, and don't worry about anything else."

Mikhail might screw it up, but there was nothing else to do; the Basmachi would not fall for it if the counter-gang didn't look like a real gang.

A squad of thirty people was organized within a few days. Most of them were Komsomol members; each knew what to do.

Their task was to gain the trust of the Basmachi and to neutralize them. Mikhail wore a Kazakh shapan (robe) and seemed to be just another bandit, but everyone in the squad listened to and obeyed him.

Armed with weapons, the newly formed bandits went around the villages, robbing mostly middle-income peasants and activists and ambushing travelers on the roads.

However, the shrewd Basmachi leader, Karakoz, had his own spies and thought the new gang seemed suspicious. On a hunch, he sent a message to the regional center, stating that the SPD chief was supporting hired bandits.

Azel's fate was decided in one day. He was contacted by the regional center and was accused of working with the bandits. He knew that no explanation would be accepted, and he could not mention Mikhail's involvement.

In despair, Azel was forced to say that the new gang was actually Karakoz's people. As SPD chief, he guaranteed that he would finish off the gang within a week.

Things were looking bad. If the members of the contrived gang were captured alive, they would tell all during the first interrogation. That would obviously be bad for Azel. But if they were all killed, his hands would be clean. He could say they were shot in the crossfire; there would be no questioning the dead.

A man, sent by Azel, came to the gang and ordered them to meet in the sands near Ayagoz. Mikhail realized what was going to happen; that night, he packed two horses with stolen goods, and that was the last anyone saw of him. On the meeting day, soldiers came and shot the sleeping bandits point-blank. Then they buried them all in one pit.

Azel told the regional center the gang had been destroyed.

Most of those thirty people were Komsomol members. Their names and the reasons for their sacrifice have been lost to oblivion. But while villainy is fleeting, the truth is eternal. An old woman living in Shymkent knows some of their names, and she always mentions them in her prayers.

Reflections

It is not easy to erase the ideas of Communism and Socialism from the mind. That may be the reason why Communists have lately begun to actively intervene in and try to influence some political events. It would be inexcusable to underestimate them.

Communism is based on religious traditions. Lenin's Bolsheviks exchanged one religion for another.[12] If they had declared that they wanted to build a society with no religion, they would have had no support. Instead, they propagated a religion of godless people.

Atheism itself is a godless religion. Battles against the church were fought with religious methods. Instead of a faith in God, they installed a belief in an idea.

Communist ways, based on Communist ideas and morals, were introduced far and wide, replacing church ceremonies and rituals. Admittedly, crime, vandalism, and theft decreased. The proletarian dictatorship established strict order; with fire and sword it eliminated any nonconformity, any attempt to break the commandments of the new religion. The Russian philosopher Nikolai Berdyaev (1874-1948) wrote about that:

---

[12] EN: On this point, see esp. Shoshana Keller, *To Moscow, Not Mecca: The Soviet Campaign against Islam in Central Asia, 1917-1941* (Praeger, 2001); cf. also David Shenk, "Marxism," in *Global Gods: Exploring the Role of Religions in Modern Societies* (Herald Press, 1995) and Christopher Dawson, "Karl Marx and the Dialectic of History," in *The Dynamics of World History*, ed. J.J. Mulloy (ISI Books, 2002), pp. 369-380.

Communism has a healthy, accurate understanding of the role of each person, largely agreeing with Christianity, which is to serve suprapersonal purposes, serving not oneself but a greater entity. However, this accurate idea is distorted by denial of the individual value and worth of each human person, his spiritual freedom. Communism is also based on the correct idea that a man is destined to unite with other people in order to regulate and organize social and cosmic life. However, this idea in Russian communism, which found its most radical expression in the words of the Christian philosopher N. [Nikolai] Fedorov, took almost maniacal forms, transforming a man into a weapon or tool of the revolution.[13]

In other words, according to Berdyaev, there are both similarities and differences between Communist morals and Christianity. Nowadays, the similarities are influencing people's minds. Everyone who votes for Communists consciously or unconsciously perceives that similarity. For Bolshevik's, the idea was God. Faith in the idea equaled fanaticism. That is why all revolutionists were fanatics who fervently believed in the idea of Communism; they were prepared to sacrifice their lives for it.

It is remarkable how persistent that idea is in the consciousness of people. From the earliest times, the human spirit has been defined by religious content. Thus it is no surprise that Lenin's idea was absorbed by the Russian people. It was the masses, the ignorant, who supported the revolution. Intellectuals joined either under a delusion, or in despair, or with a desire to make a name for themselves. However, the creative intellectuals, for the most part, did not support the revolution.

The books *The Life of Klim Samgin,* by Maxim Gorky, and *Doctor Zhivago,* by Boris Pasternak, told stories of the troubling searches, spiritual turmoil, and discord among the intellectuals—what they had to endure.

Russian intellectuals understood the discrepancies between Communist ideas and Christian commandments, and therefore they opposed the ideas of Communism.

The nightmare of Bolshevist morals is that such morals turn people into tools of destruction, annihilation, and decay. Indeed, it is well known that the machinery of government disposed of innocent people, that many of them were

---

[13] N. A. Berdyaev, *Origins and Meaning of Russian Communism*, reprint (Moscow, 1990), pp. 125–126.

arrested, exiled, executed, and tormented in the torture chambers of the NKVD (the People's Commissariat for Internal Affairs).

It was the war of religions. Humankind had not invented anything new.

The Communist ideology was fundamentally a religious ideology. I do not doubt that the next generation will evaluate Communism as such, just as all previous revolutionary slogans as well as social, political, and economic factors have disappeared like foam.

Come to think of it, how can one become rich by taking wealth from others? What was the sense in all the changes and revolutionary perturbations if they made everyone immediately poor? It is obvious that the claims that first everyone needs to be made poor to be equal, or to make everyone equal, they first need to be made poor, are absurd.

Communism came to Kazakhstan through forced and missionary means. At first, we learned of Communism at gunpoint. Then when the repressions started, we accepted it out of fear, and thus, we became Communists. Communism put down roots; it grew strong and firmly established in the Russian land. In this regard, I refer to the words of Berdyaev once again,

> "Russian Communism under closer analysis in the context of the Russian historic fate, contains a deformation of the Russian idea, Russian messianism and universalism, the Russian search for the tsardom of truth, the Russian idea that took unsightly forms in an atmosphere of war and decay. Yet Russian communism is more linked to Russian traditions than is usually thought, however, they were not only good traditions, but very bad ones as well" (ibid., pp. 148–151).

Other nations should be discussed more carefully, but here is what seems evident and indisputable: Communists accomplished a passionate leap, based on the Russian idea, and this passionate leap combined with the new, Communist religion of atheism. As a result, Communism became the backbone of the Russian idea and helped it to become a decisive world force. Everyone understands that the once proclaimed Socialist camp is the dwelling space for the Russian idea. That is why it is very hard to erase the ideas of Socialism and Communism from memory, because they can change form and reappear and successfully thrive in our lives.

Sometimes I wonder, How could Communists challenge all other religions, and then so quickly, in such a short time, create their own? Today, there are still many people who cannot escape that question.

Socialism was an atheistic society. University seniors took a course called *Principles of Scientific Atheism*. One of the key elements of atheism was the negation and subversion of religions. The Communists that participated in funerals or other traditions and rituals were severely punished. However, Socialism could not defeat religion. Because religion is the essence of human nature, it is impossible to destroy it. I want to tell you a story told to me once by the elderly Beysen.

The Elderly Beysen's Story

Fifteen-year-old Amina was terminally ill. She was unconscious. Her parents, pale and tearful, sat at her bedside; they felt the end was coming near, but they did not say that to each other. There was nothing they could do.

The girl's father, a harsh man once, was glancing at his wife questioningly, his arms hanging limply. It seemed the only pillar and hope left for him was his ever calm and quiet wife. He looked at her with imploring eyes. What would they do if the girl woke up again and repeated the request that had put him in such dismay that he was pouring with sweat. He had to wipe his face with his sleeve over and over again.

His wife glanced at him and thought, "Poor man, it must be hard for him to see his little girl in such a state."

But Muktash was lost for other reasons. At midday, when his wife was puttering around the fire making lunch, the girl had suddenly told him, "Father, remember when Grandpa died, a mullah came and said a prayer. I want to hear it."

Muktash got scared; he thought that she must have been delirious, nothing else. The mullah had already forgotten his way to them. Even that time for Grandpa, Muktash had invited the mullah only out of fear that people would judge him.

If he could have it his way, the mullah would not be allowed near his daughter. Muktash did not like mullahs very much; he was a true atheist. Mullahs knew him as well and kept away from his house.

His wife used to start making flatbreads and would ask him to call a mullah to say a prayer and commemorate the souls of the deceased ancestors, but Muktash would get angry and swing at her, "None of that nonsense. Don't you have anything better to do?" His wife knew her husband's temper and stopped asking.

Muktash's state was understandable, then, when his own daughter, the family's favorite, suddenly wanted to hear a prayer. But when she got better and joined the Komsomol, what would she tell her comrades? He would throw such a big feast then. He would gather everyone so they could be happy for his daughter.

He remembered how he had joined the Komsomol. He was not just a member, but an activist. He launched a battle against class enemies, against mullahs. There was even a saying in the village, "When Muktash walks by, even babies do not dare to cry, out of fear." He was still known as an avid Communist. So how could it happen that his own flesh and blood said words so indecent for a Communist's daughter.

Amina calmed a bit and started searching for her father's hand. Muktash took her hands into his palms and felt her fever. His heart sank with an ominous premonition. His daughter turned her head and peered at her father. She had grown up to be such a beauty! Her big black eyes pierced right into his heart.

Muktash did not notice his tears, he was so woeful. It was the first time his wife had ever seen him cry. "My goodness, he is being torn up by grief," she thought. Suddenly her thoughts were interrupted by the drawn but fretful voice of her daughter, "Father, I want to hear the mullah. They have a prayer for disease."

Muktash went pale and thought, "Why does she talk about that? If she had said those words when she was well, I could have yelled at her. But what can I tell her now."

The silence was broken by his wife, "Daughter, the mullah makes communion and prays for the sick to get better."

"That is what I need," the girl said harshly.

Muktash gave in and called for the mullah. As soon as the mullah started saying, "*La ilaha illallah (There is no god but God). . .*" Amina interrupted him, "Grandpa, teach me this prayer. I want to say it myself."

The mullah repeated the prayer several times. Amina memorized it and started muttering it to herself. The mullah took her hand, checking her pulse, then went white as a sheet. The mother understood that Amina was dying. "Insha'Allah. Insha'Allah (God's will be done, God's will be done)," mumbled the scared mullah. The girl could barely move her lips, but she was saying her own requiem. That evening she died. The mullah was sitting at her feet weeping. Muktash had never seen him cry before.

Seven days after the death of his daughter, Muktash came to the mullah's house. The following conversation took place between them:

"Come in, Muktash. Have a seat."

"Moldeke, don't be scared. I came to you with a request."

"Tell me. I will help you if I can."

"Moldeke, teach me how to pray. I want to chant a requiem for her until the fortieth day memorial.[14] I once knew it as a child, but I have forgotten." Then he started crying. The mullah looked at the crying atheist in confusion.

Reflections

I met Muktash. He passed away only recently and was buried next to his daughter, whom people called Holy Amina. Until his death, he performed Salah (prayer) and was known as a devout person. I had not known that he once was an avid atheist.

---

[14] EN: Central Asian Muslims, including the Kazakhs, observe memorials on the seventh, fortieth and one-year mark after someone's death; the third and 100th days are also at times observed. See esp. Bruce Privratsky, "The Funeral Cycle and Memorial Feast," in *Muslim Turkistan: Kazak Religion and Collective Memory* (Routledge, 2001), pp. 141-145.

CHAPTER 3
COLLAPSE OF THE SOCIALIST CAMP

The disease of Socialism is inborn. Its collapse conforms to the laws of history. Those who anticipated this collapse were declared enemies and were destroyed by Communist ideologists. For the most part, Kazakh intellectuals did not accept Socialism. Therefore, they became outcasts and class enemies, enemies of people. Bloody repressions started immediately, from the very first days of constructing the Socialist community.

Reflections

The Socialist society is built on faith. That faith is based on ideas of Communism. It is faith without God. Pure faith may annihilate the humane. How can a heart not harden when it is taught to be ready for battle, to destroy other people by proclaiming them to be enemies?

What could be the sense in having a son turn against his father, with the only explanation being that it was his duty within the Communist idea? According to Bolshevist ideology, faith is stronger than family ties. If your loved ones do not share that idea with you, they are your enemies. Although such beliefs have certainly occurred before on an individual or local level, the phenomenon of introducing such manner of thinking universally, on a scale of mass proportions, is very rare in history.

The Soviet regime installed such morals, which slowly became the key principles for constructing Socialist society. New ideas that complied with the new ideology appeared. Such principles were systematized and formulated in the Communist morality.

On October 2, 1920, during the Third Youth Congress, Vladimir Lenin expanded the goals and tasks of the Komsomol and established their political essence in his lecture "The Tasks of the Youth Leagues." Millions of copies of that speech were circulated throughout the entire country. Every Pioneer, every Komsomol member, was honor bound to memorize Lenin's words by heart.

In his speech, Lenin discussed the specifics of Communist morality, extensively and explicitly. He indicated that the most important area of work for the Youth Leagues was to educate the young in the spirit of Communist morality.

"Dawn," by K.T. Telzhanov, 1970. Courtesy of the A. Kasteev State Museum of Arts (Almaty, Kazakhstan).

What did Communist morality mean? To answer this question, Lenin borrowed from two key concepts of Marxism discussing morality in regard to class positions and in regard to political principles. In this context, morality lost its original connotation and acquired features of a political phenomenon.

Lenin divided morality into two types: Communistic and bourgeois. He severely criticized the latter because, as he claimed, capitalist society was based on faith in God, on suppressing one's humanity. Lenin said, "We do not believe in God, and we shall not allow religion, like a leech, to suck the blood of the working people."

Thus Lenin defined the main idea: people should not follow God's path; this could not be allowed in any circumstance! Only atheists were worthy of respect.

That thought contradicted ideas of humanity established through the centuries. According to the ancient Greeks, "Man is the measure of all things." Humanism teaches that, regardless of religion, race, eye shape, or wealth, humans, as such, are the highest achievement of nature, its pinnacle.

If we agree and accept this humanistic definition, we cannot see a religious person as fulfilled. Our humanity is what unites everyone on earth, despite any ideological dispute.

Why should a religious person be an enemy? Where does that take us? Bolshevism indeed did not bring any new ideology. Its only difference from the traditional ideology was in its godlessness, in its negation of God. It is the religion of godless men, a religion of the crowd.

Immediately after seizing power, Bolsheviks realized that they would not achieve anything without a new religion. They had to form and present an artificially created God. Bolsheviks reinforced propaganda and campaigning in that direction. The image of Marx, the champion of the proletariat, was presented to everyone, instead of God. Upon Lenin's death, Stalin attempted to create a "God" out of the deceased leader. He succeeded to a certain degree.

Throughout the past seventy years, Lenin's renown has been on a level with that of prophets. This begs the question, What have people achieved by following Lenin? Everybody has his or her own answer.

****

In the 1960s, the Communists, headed by Khrushchev, reduced the idea of Communism to an absurdity. A specific example of that is the Third Party Program adopted at the 22nd congress of Communists in 1961, which ratified the moral code for the constructors of Communism. The content of the moral code was devotion to the cause of Communism and ardent love and devotion to the Socialist Motherland. The program also specified the exact date for the construction of Communism—1980. We talked with enthusiasm about how we were fortunate to live under Communism. But what is Communism?

> Communism is a classless social system with one form of public ownership of the means of production and with full social equality for all members of society. Under communism, the all-around development of people will be accompanied by the growth of the productive forces based on continuous progress in science and technology. All the springs of social wealth will flow abundantly, and the great principle, 'From each according to his ability, to each according to his needs' will be implemented. Communism is a highly organized society of free, socially conscious working people, a society in which public self-government will be established, a society in which labor for the good of society will become the prime vital requirement for everyone, a clearly recognized necessity, and the ability of each person will be employed to the greatest benefit of the people.[15]

It would be reasonable and fair to call the 1960s the years of political madness. In those years one could hear many insane slogans and invocations that would never occur in the mind of a rational person. In this regard, the storyline in the Abai Qunanbaiuli's poem "The Legend of Azim" comes to my mind.

Khidr came to Azim in his dream and said that it would rain soon, and people would go mad from the rainwater. Azim had to tell the tsar. The tsar, his vizier, and Azim put in stores of pure water as a reserve.

When the rain started, the people went mad and revolted against the tsar, "He does not understand us. The tsar and his attendants are mad; they need to be killed."

---

[15] *The 22nd Congress of the Communist Party of the Soviet Union, 17–31 October 1961: Verbatim Records.* 3 Vols (Moscow, 1962), vol. 3, p. 274.

The tsar asked Azim for advice. Azim replied, "We can do nothing else but drink the maddening water and become the same as the crowd."

They drank the rainwater, and when people saw that they were doing the same as them, they were glad and said, "Now they are finally like us."

The situation in the 1960s was like that story. On the one hand, people began to come round, after Stalin's repressions. On the other hand, they were years of organized social madness for constructing Communism in the country, which had a pitiable and submarginal economy.

I was talking to the elderly Beysen. I recalled Khrushchev's fantasies that, in 1980, the era of Communism would start in the USSR.

I asked the old man, "Some people claim that we had Communism, but now it is gone. What would you say to that?"

"My friend, I have never seen Communism in my life, since I don't even know what it is. It could be true—that's what the knowledgeable people say."

"But still..." I insisted.

"What should I do with you? OK, I will tell you one funny story."

In the 1980s, when everyone was ecstatically and enthusiastically expecting the announcement that Communism had been constructed, a propaganda lecturer came to our area to explain what to expect under Communism.

He used the word "Communism" over and over again in his lecture. Finally, he ended his speech with, "The onset of Communism is near; it is right there on the horizon."

An old man listened to the lecture then went home and asked his student son, "Son, a lecturer came and talked about Communism. He said it is on the horizon. What is a horizon anyway?"

His son was late for his date, so he gave a short reply, "How can I explain that to you, Father? Basically, a horizon is the place that you will never reach, no matter how long you walk."

The old man brightened up, "Oh, thank you, son. Now it's all clear to me."

I had heard that joke before, but it sounded different coming from the elderly Beysen.

If Marx called Communism a specter, then that joke made it into an illusion. I was born in that society, in that illusion, and I lived in it.

To study Hegel's dialectics, to understand Marx's philosophy while living in that illusion was like a breath of fresh air for me. Even though a sensible man now understands that those teachings offered nothing of significance after all.

Back in his day, Lenin said, "Dialectics is the soul of Marxism." It was the most precise and complete definition for Communist propaganda and Bolshevist policy. Both dialectics and Marxism were highly desirable for Communists. These two systems came to us from Europe. To clarify this matter, I will talk first about Marxism. As the name suggests, Marxism is associated with Marx's theory.

In the 1970s and 1980s, Soviet scientists who considered themselves to be free of Marxism, wrote that Karl Marx and Marxism were different ideas that should be studied separately, as Marx himself was opposed to calling his theory by his own name.

They did not allow any criticism of Marx but pretended to criticize those who hid behind Marxism. It could have been true. Perhaps Marx could not be blamed for everything that was piled up in Marxism. However, it was Marx who formulated the main principles of his theory. Therefore, Marxism cannot exist separately from its author. As the saying goes, "You cannot throw out the words of a song."

Karl Marx was an academic economist. In his works, he dealt with many issues. He published some historical papers as well. Marxist philosophers wrote multiple works on his philosophic and economic papers. Karl Marx attempted to understand the entire world and humankind in his books, but he researched history only from the positions of atheism and European thinking.

Marx was an atheist scientist from Western Europe. He did not account for historic ontology in his works. It would be erroneous for us to think that he was a scientist who attempted to solve societal problems in general.

Not a single speech or article in Soviet times could avoid citing Marx and his theory. In this fashion, Marxism had become a thinking methodology in Socialist society. Lenin wrote an entire article explaining the key principles and ideas of Marxism.

According to Lenin, Marxism had three sources and three components: First, Marx's system of economic knowledge was based on ideas from the English classical economists Adam Smith and David Ricardo. Second, his idea of scientific communism came from his study of French utopists, such as Saint-Simon (Claude Henri de Rouvroy, comte de Saint-Simon) and Charles Fourier. Third, the Marxist philosophy was based on the German classical philosophies of Immanuel Kant, Georg Hegel, and others.

Higher-education schools taught Marxism as a mandatory discipline. The first year included a course in the history of the Communist Party; the second year included Marxist-Leninist philosophy, which consisted of dialectic and historical materialism; and the third year included a class on political economies of both capitalism and Socialism. Seniors studied principles of scientific communism and scientific atheism. All of these courses were social disciplines in the service of Communist ideology.

Since independence, these subjects have gradually disappeared from academic programs, but their traces still remain. In the period of triumph for Communist ideas, during Khrushchev's administration, the only subject with intellectual potential was Marxist-Leninist philosophy. Forward-minded teachers did not tie this course to Marx or Lenin. Instead, they taught the history of world philosophy, from ancient Greece to the twentieth century, as an introduction to philosophy. Dialectic materialism was the most difficult to digest, but still, the course forced students to cultivate the culture and skills of logical thinking. In this context, the famous saying, "Dialectics is the soul of Marxism," was justified, with regard to the development of logical thinking.

Dialectics originates from the Greek Socratic "dialogue." Hegel was one of those who wanted to formulate the systematic teaching of dialectics. As I mentioned earlier, Hegel's philosophy became one of the cornerstones of Marxism and was considered the pinnacle of world philosophy. The study of Hegel's legacy gained the status of a philosophical problem. A full campaign was initiated in this regard. If you had mastered Hegel's dialectics, you were considered an expert in philosophy in general. Studying Hegel's teachings, through Lenin's Philosophical Notebooks, became essential.

Indeed, it was not an easy task to study and master Hegel's teachings; he was a complex scientist who chose not to explain everything in simple and comprehensible terms, preferring instead to confuse and sidetrack readers. That principle was obligatory for Hegel, who was a mystic philosopher. His theory of the idea, in its time, had a positive effect on the formation and development of philosophical thinking in Kazakhstan. However, the greatest downside of Hegel's philosophy was that his teaching completely disregarded humans, their feelings, their emotions, and their inner essence. Hegel's philosophy is the logic of pure thinking.

What then is dialectics? Why did Lenin call it the soul of Marxism? At that time, the adherents of dialectics liked to repeat Lenin's claim; yet now, when Marxism is no longer on the agenda, they do not find this statement appropriate anymore.

Dialectics is a theory of development, a process that requires tendencies and opposing forces. This struggle results in development and progress, which was what attracted Marx and, especially, Lenin. They used it as a means for class struggle. For revolutionaries, dialectics became an irreplaceable way to search for actual enemies and, most of all, to create artificial ones. In this way, materialistic dialectics provided the basis for the new philosophy.

Friedrich Engels, in his book Anti-Dühring, wrote that dialectics had three laws: the law of the unity and struggle of opposites, the law of transition from quantity to quality, and the law of negation of the negation. Thus he transformed the philosophy into a mathematics multiplication table. These notions, known since Aristotle's time, had suddenly become the ideas and categories of dialectics. Thus, the discipline of dialectic materialism was established. That discipline does not exist anymore, but it has been partially preserved in the discipline of philosophy; therefore, we cannot say that it has disappeared entirely.

Lenin, and later, Stalin applied dialectics in practice, thus dooming people to unforeseen torments and sufferings. The ideas of the class enemy and the enemy of the people were fruits of the dialectic doctrine.

I have no doubts that Marxist-Leninist philosophy, with its chapters on dialectic and historical materialism, were a system of knowledge created with the specific task of serving Communist ideology. Lenin used the history of philosophy to derive the Party principle and then propagated it in every possible way. Certainly, it does seem ludicrous now. Representatives of dialectic materialism were militant materialists. In their constant search for enemies, they did not reflect on consensus, agreement, or truce.

Old people used to say, "Fear those who do not fear God." Bolsheviks feared no God. Indeed, they deemed it disgraceful to talk of God or even to admit His existence; thus the subject was closed.

The semiliterate Khrushchev came to power and started tightening the screws. "Under Communism, no one should have any personal property" was the slogan under which livestock was taken away from people who had accumulated domestic animals. A camel was declared unsuitable and useless for a farmstead. All camels were given to meat processing plants or to households, for slaughtering. A standard was later set: it was permissible to keep no more than one cow or horse, and five or six sheep. This was wrong, but local administrations zealously rushed to execute the order. In those evil times, I witnessed the incident below.

It is impossible to retell everything. However, one thing can be asserted unequivocally: the social society we had created had no respect for men of merit. They were humiliated, persecuted, tried, exiled, executed, labeled, fired, and blacklisted.

Misfortunes and troubles befell not only humans; animals suffered as well. During those years we lost camels and horses. Camel husbandry was erased from all government programs, plans, and reports. The number of horses dropped dramatically.

My Story

One could talk about it forever, but one thing was true: the life of a freethinker was not easy in Socialist society. Some were judged; others were anathematized, exiled, or executed.

Despite the difficult postwar years, by the 1960s the number of households began to increase, the amount of family-owned livestock grew, and people started to thaw; it seemed their suffering was over. However, the government was on the lookout. Khrushchev's doctrine emerged, claiming that Communism would be established everywhere in 1980. That meant that any excessive livestock had to be taken away to eradicate any private-ownership interests. There was a standard tradition during Soviet times: if an order came from above, it had to be not just fulfilled, but exceeded.

The folk saying goes, "Teach a fool to bow with grace, and he will fall flat on his face." Thus, zealous local activists hurried to execute orders.

One little Kazakh village offered resistance to the construction of Communism. It was a bold action by one man, Yerkebay. The administration allowed each household to own one cow and four heads of smaller livestock. However, Yerkebay had an extra animal, a jet-black horse that he had raised and prepared for races. The village council demanded that he give the horse up for meat, but Yerkebay flatly refused. Eventually, a district-center official was called.

Who could ever stay indifferent to the word *baiga* (horse race)?

As a kid, I often heard, "Ah, is there any horse equal to Yerkebay's jet black stallion!" and "That horse runs like the wind!"

There was even a Kazakh saying, "Erkebaiding baige karakogi," which meant "Yerkebay's black racer."

That horse made its owner famous. I saw the black colt. In those times, they always organized horse races for the November 7 holiday celebrating the Great October Socialist Revolution.[16] It may seem of little consequence now, but when you suddenly saw riders on horses barreling around the corner, you felt something incomparable. The teen rider, lying tight against the withers of the black horse, would loosen the reins just before the finish line. The horse, which had been restrained by the bit, would suddenly transform. It seemed his hooves did not touch the ground, and he was flying through the air, weightless and swift.

Unfortunately, that famous racer was an extra for Yerkebay's household, and thus, it became an obstacle in the construction of Communism.

The district administrator and his assistant went to see Yerkebay.

The administrator said, "We came to you on business. Now is not the time for friendly visits."

Yerkebay asked, "What's the hurry? One should take a moment to enjoy the time gifted to you by the Creator. Life flies by as fast as a running horse."

"That's enough, Yereke. There's no need to teach me. I carry out the policies of the Party and the government. The bottom line is, you need to give up your excessive livestock."

"What excessive livestock?" Yereke asked. I have one cow, four sheep."

His eyes blazing, the officer said, "Did you forget about that black horse you keep for races? Or is it not your horse?"

"My friend, you grew up here. You know the black racer is not just mine; he's everybody's pet. He brings joy to everyone."

---

[16] EN: The Revolution occurred on October 24-25, 1917 according to the Julian calendar which was employed at the time. It was November 7 according to the Gregorian calendar, which was put into effect in February 1918.

"Save your breath. That's nonsense. So the black racer's victories are yours, but the horse is not?"

"It's no use trying to explain it to you. If you're too stupid to understand who his owner really is, there's nothing I can do. While I am alive, I will not give up the black racer for meat, and I will not allow people like you to even touch him."

Yerkebay stood up, signaling an end to the conversation.

The officer, red with anger, got up as well. "You are resisting authority."

"I doubt my horse will get in the way of your construction of Communism," Yerkebay said.

After lunch, the administrator came back. This time he brought Officer Yerden with him.

"Yereke," the officer said, "you better give up the horse voluntarily; otherwise, we'll have to take it by force. Bring out the horse. You can get money for it from the administration."

"You think you can take my horse away by force?" Yerkebay flew into a rage. In the blink of an eye he dashed to the wall, grabbed his shotgun, and even managed to load it.

Officer Yerden was glad to see this turn of events; it played right into his hands. He thought, "Now we've got you, my friend. Now you can kiss your horse good-bye, and you may lose your head, too, for drawing a gun on authorities."

Yerden said, "How have you hidden your hostile nature for so long, Yereke. We'll just have to continue our conversation in a different environment. I'll be back tomorrow. Good-bye."

Yerkebay sat at home, lost and in shock. He knew trouble was coming, and he blamed himself for grabbing his gun in anger, for losing control. In the 1930s, his older brother had been declared an enemy of the people and was exiled to Siberia. He never returned.

"Yes, you are playing with fire, Yereke," he said bitterly.

Yerkebay could not sleep; he tossed and turned all night. What could he do, just accept it and give up his favorite horse up for meat? How good could the meat of a racing horse be? It would be all tendons. They must know that. Though, if all administrators were like the guy from yesterday, with no brains or compassion, what could he expect from them?

Yerkebay was not a person for deep thoughts; he always tried to stop himself from thinking too much. He felt that if he allowed his thoughts free rein, they might take him too far. He did not like most of the village and district administrators. They seemed shallow, like autumn puddles. What would happen to the nation with such people in charge? What would its future be?

People had just started to raise their heads again after the postwar years. They had just started to turn their lives around, to live, if not prosperously, at least not starving. But then the new trouble arrived.

On every corner, they had started complaining about surpluses. They were having all kinds of conversations about fairness. Why was the Party quiet? Did its leaders agree with this new group that was gaining power? If so, what would our lives be about?

Yerkebay tried to drive the worrisome questions out of his head. This time though, they were firmly stuck and refused to go away. He struggled to think of any answers. He had only one consolation—his black horse, which had brought him glory and happiness. Now they were trying to take away that happiness. They must have thought that it was too good for him. So they crowded around, hissing at him to send the horse to slaughter.

But people needed the black racer; he was an attraction at any holiday or celebration. Why couldn't they understand that?

"Is it my fault that I have a racing horse? I am not a wealthy man. I'm not a mullah. I haven't harmed anyone. What is my guilt?"

His wife saw him suffering and tried to console him, "Try to sleep, at least for a little bit. What shall be, shall be. Just accept it. Inshallah."

She was wise and talked little. Yerkebay liked how she could understand him quickly and always took his side. "Yes, if people like her were in power, life would be different," Yerkebay thought with appreciation.

His wife continued to soothe him, carefully choosing her words.

Yerkebay got up early, as usual, and fed and watered the horse. He wanted to get him ready for the October (November 7) holiday's race, to try his luck.

The morning light shined on the horse's coat, glistening from navy blue to jet-black. "How can I give up such a thoroughbred for meat? They are twits," he thought angrily. Deep in his thoughts, he did not notice the police chief, Kusen, arriving, along with Officer Yerden and the administrator from yesterday.

Yerkebay's heart sank, anticipating trouble. It was obvious that it would not be easy to get rid of them.

"Yereke, you had some time to think. We came for the horse." The administrator ordered Officer Yerden, "Bring out the horse."

Yerden looked at Yerkebay and cautiously stepped closer to the horse.

Yerkebay stood still as a stone, as if no force could move him. Hopelessness and despair, detachment and apathy to everything happening around him overwhelmed Yerkebay.

The administrator handed him a small slip of paper. It was a receipt for delivering livestock for meat.

Stretching out his hand, Yerkebay took the paper automatically. It would have ended there, but suddenly his wife came running out of the house with the shotgun. Yerkebay's face changed color. Now he understood what his wife was telling him last night. Yes, it could be God's will.

He took the shotgun. "I am sorry my poor friend. It's better for you to die of my bullet than to accept a shameful death from the enemy." He mumbled those words, took aim, and pulled the trigger. The bullets hit directly in the horse's heart.

Yes, it could not have happened any other way—before every race, Yerkebay would put his ear against the horse's big chest and count it's heartbeats. He had tried to teach his horse to breathe evenly and deeply. That day, he had to cut short the trained breathing of the black stallion.

The horse dropped on the spot. His legs twitched for a short time, and soon he grew quiet.

Chief Kusen had not expected that; he blinked, dumbfounded, then looked at the administrator and nodded, as if saying it was time to go. They left.

The administrator wrote in his report that the order was fulfilled; the population had no excessive livestock.

Yerkebay and his wife stood by the prostrate horse, not saying a single word.

Reflections

In the late 1970s and early 1980s, Socialism began to recede. Some noticed, but others did not. Those who lived well, who had managed to settle well, certainly did not want to change anything. They only wanted things to stay the same. Others, whose life was not as easy, started to see failures in the Socialist system; they understood that changes were bound to happen.

It was a competition between capitalism and Socialism. Communists increased their public propaganda, more each day. They held gatherings, here and there, and delivered lectures about the victorious march of Communism.

The elderly Beysen remembered one such occasion:

Once, after another lecture, the writer Gabit Musrepov, who was in the audience, asked the lecturer a question: "They say we will catch up with America. Is that true, my friend?"

"Yes, we won't just catch up with it, we'll surpass it."

"We might catch up, perhaps, but I think we shouldn't try to outrun it."

"Why is that?"

"Then they will see our bare behinds." That was the answer.

****

The first time I heard that Socialism would grind to a halt was from Grandpa Yesim. Once, at the table he had said, "This government will not go far. I won't see it. You," he nodded at my father, "will only see the beginning, but your son will live in those times."

That was what my grandpa said in 1961, after he found out that Khrushchev had ordered the removal of Stalin's body from Lenin's Mausoleum.

One of us asked, "Yeseke, why do you say that?"

Grandpa Yesim coughed and said, "When a government starts persecuting itself, it means the regime will not last for long."

Indeed, both Stalin and Khrushchev were representatives of the same political system, but they were opponents and enemies as well.

The downfall of Stalin meant the collapse of the pillars of Socialism. Grandfather understood that even then. That thought suddenly engulfed me when I was standing before Chairman Mao's portrait in Tiananmen Square in Beijing. Was it not Mao who flooded China with blood during the Cultural Revolution? Yes, the public replied, but Mao was the founder of Chinese national identity; he was an outstanding political leader. I heard those words later as well, not only in Beijing, but also in many other corners of the Celestial Empire.

To move forward, you must not destroy everything from the past. This thought did not occur to Khrushchev. Thus, by stripping Stalin of his father-of-the-nation status, he started to lose his own name, as well.

It was the beginning of the collapse of Socialism.

Sitting at a dastarkhan in a regular village house, you can hear things that never occur to those in power. Answers to the most complicated questions may be found among common people. The problem is only to find such pearls of national wisdom, to hear them and comprehend them.

The government has a certain power of creation. Everyone who comes to power should understand that he or she is not the rule, but has only been given a chance to access it. Future generations and historians will tell how past rulers came to power and what kind of ruler they were. Political leaders can be truly known only after they leave office. As for Khrushchev, even though he was in power, he could not prove himself as a leader.

No matter how despotic Stalin has been, no matter what we have said about him, it is impossible to claim that he was not a successful political leader. He was a tyrant, an executioner, but he was able to use his power; that fact cannot be ignored. The same goes for Mao.

Adolf Hitler, on the other hand, was only an opportunist who had maneuvered his way into the upper levels of government. He could not be a real political leader. He humiliated his nation, made it kneel before the court of history. He was a pathetic character, a criminal who committed cruel and unforgivable wrongs.

Socialism has disappeared into the snows of yesteryear. The past seems like a terrible nightmare. When we relive memories of those years, we understand how amoral the situation was for common citizens. People carried out orders from above and did only as instructed. There was no other way. If you take a closer look, it becomes clear that, for all those years, people lived as if under a microscope. Now this complicated period of history seems only a scary dream, but that dream was their reality.

My Story

In Socialist society, there was an institution responsible for propaganda—the "Knowledge" Society. Under orders from the regional Knowledge Society office, we went to the district center, "K," to give lectures to the general public. There were two lecturers: a historian, Sagdat, who had a pendulous lower lip and would always interrupt with questions in all the wrong places, and me. Our companions were the head of the Knowledge Society's district office and "M," a respectable old man who accompanied us on his way home.

"My friend, how soon will we get to the village?" Sagdat asked, not knowing whom to pester.

"Patience, my friend. We're coming up to Kara Olgen now, so only two more hours. God willing, we'll be there by lunch," M replied.

"'Kara Olgen', '(The place where) the Black (army) Died'"—that's quite a name," Sagdat said. "We have a place called '(The Place where) the Bull Died' in our area. It would have been better to call the place 'the Cow Died' since the Kazakhs call a cow *kara* (black)."

The old man looked disapprovingly at Sagdat, whom he had immediately disliked. I also felt a slight disaffection for him.

"The name has its own story," said the head of the regional Knowledge Society. He had been keeping quiet but now entered the conversation. "It means the place where Basmachi died." He grew quiet, watching the old man, as if inviting him to continue the topic.

"There's the place that the locals call Kara Olgen," the driver waved his arm.

It was evident that Sagdat's words touched a nerve for all three of us. Yes, the Kazakhs could be a bit odd in their names of localities, but they all had their reasons, their history.

"There's a cemetery there, and over there was a house," the driver pointed somewhere, but I did not notice anything. The old man quietly mumbled a prayer and drew his hands over his face.[17] The driver repeated the same ritual.

The silence was broken by the old man. "It is my fault that I brought up this subject. If you are willing, I can tell you the story behind the name for this place. I'm sorry if my story is incomplete; I can only tell what I remember. I am not really a man of words. But whenever I pass this place, I always remember what once happened here. I try to never travel here alone; I always feel ill at ease. It's not that I am scared, no. I am not the scared type" he said pointing at a deep scar on his face (he had obviously experienced war). "But I still feel emotional. Of course, I do not pity the bandit Basmachi, but the innocent souls of the young people who died. When I image their death throes, my heart grows cold."

We sat motionless, listening to the old man. Our attention encouraged him, and he started his story.

The Old Man's Story

When people split into two camps, there were builders of the new happy life, and those who were in favor of reinstituting the old regime. They both took to arms to defend their interests, whereas the common village people were completely confused: Who was right; who was wrong? Whom they should hide from; whom should they fraternize with? Their beliefs, which had been developed over centuries, had collapsed. New ideas about bad wealthy peasants or herdsmen and good humble peasants or herdsmen had developed. To be known as good, you had to have absolutely nothing. If you owned even a trifle, it was as good as lost. Judgment days came to wealthy people. Peasants of medium and high welfare were dispossessed and exiled. But that was not the end. Armed bandits robbed common people, took their last belongings, raped and murdered them, burned their houses.

The old man's story was about those times.

Impatient Sagdat quipped, "So what side were you on? When you talk about armed bandits, do you mean the soldiers of the Red Army?"

---

[17] This is common practice when Central Asian Muslims pass by a place where deceased ancestors, holy men or national heroes are buried. See again Privratsky, *Muslim Turkistan*.

The old man quietly looked at me. I encouraged him, "Go on, we are listening."

During those years, people with guns were divided into the Reds, the Whites, and the Blacks. I did not know why, but those who took up rifles and went against the local authorities were called Blacks. Possibly, it was because of their black deeds.

There were five armed bandits. Their head was the bloodsucker, Salt-Akhmet; two of them were Russian Kazakhs, as they were called among the people. It is scary to think of what they did during those years. They especially persecuted those who joined a kolkhoz. They killed their livestock, burned their bee houses. Their last atrocity was when they broke into the house of a poor man, Kozhakhmet. They looted his belongings and took his daughter, Bisara, when they left.

The Cossack, Isay, had put Salt-Akhmet up to that. "Sakeh,[18] we need to take her with us. People in a kolkhoz say that they own everything in common; let Bisara be our common girlfriend."

"Right here," the old man pointed out at some hills, "Sarsen and his grandson Zhanat tended sheep."

Sarsen's daughter-in-law and son worked in the kolkhoz. They begged him to return to the kolkhoz, "You don't need to live alone on the steppe."

The old man would reply, "Have patience, I'll spend one more winter here, and then in summer I'll move in with you."

Salt-Akhmet's gang barged into Sarsen's house one evening.

Sarsen knew that trouble was coming. He did not fear for himself, but for his grandson. They might say he was the son of a kolkhoz man and kill him. "Oh God, help us and save us from misfortune," mumbled the old man.

"Here's the father of a Communist," Salt-Akhmet said with scorn. "Greet your guests, old man. Don't worry; we have a woman with us."

Sarsen recognized Kozhakhmet's daughter, Bisara, dressed in a man's clothing.

"We are always glad to have guests, but we have nothing to treat you with. We'll make some tea, though. Come in."

---

[18] This again is the shortened form of Salt-Akmet's name appended with the 'ake/eke' ending for colloquial respect.

The Cossack, Isay, looked around, dissatisfied with the host's answer. He dismounted his horse and went straight to the barn. Soon, the beheaded body of a goat landed at the old man's feet.

Salt-Ahmet smiled, "That's right, now we can have a proper feast. Come on, old man; put the meat into the pot."

They started a fire. The meat was stewing in a big pot; Sarsen and his grandson were making tea. The old man glanced worriedly at his grandson, Zhanat, "He is young; I hope he doesn't try to do anything stupid. I should have sent him to the village, but it is a long journey. What if he froze on his way or got attacked by wolves? I thought it would be better to have him near and hope that trouble would avoid us."

It would have been all right, but Isay, sated with meat and drunk on tea and the moonshine they had brought with them, suddenly got up, his eyes blazing, and said: "What should we do with these Communists, Salt-Ahmet? Why don't the Kazakhs have a cellar? Where should we put them? We can't just tie them up and leave them here—they will ruin our air, and our beauty needs fresh air, doesn't she?"

The chief replied without thinking, "Isay, put them outside. They say Communists are hardy."

"Why didn't I think of that? Old man, come out." He walked over to Zhanat and poked him in the ribs, "Go outside. We'll rest in here with our beauty."

Poor Bisara shouted, "Ata, Zhanat, don't leave. They'll kill me! I'm scared of them. Don't leave me alone, don't go!"

"Shut up, bitch!" Isay swung and hit the girl. Bisara fell, bursting into tears.

The bandits kicked the old man and his grandson outside. Sarsen only had a moment to grab his chapan. But what good would one chapan do for the two of them in the winter cold? Zhanat, with just one shirt on, was already chattering with cold.

Sarsen ran back to the house and started pounding at the door with his fists, asking the bandits to let them in, at least to a cubbyhole.

One of the bandits came out and started beating the old man. Zhanat tried to come to his aid, but was kicked in the chest. His eyes went dark, and he fell unconscious.

When he woke up, he saw his grandpa was unconscious and bleeding. In only a few minutes, Sarsen passed away in the arms of his grandson. What could the boy do? Zhanat's eyes were dry. He looked ahead, not noticing anything. He had to get to the village, to inform the villagers, but he had no strength to get up. Could he make it there anyway in such cold? He was growing numb from the cold.

He thought of his grandpa, who had told him many times that there were no hopeless situations. Suddenly, it dawned on him; he knew what he had to do. Poor Bisara was inside, but it would be better for her to die than to live in shame.

Around noon the next day, a small group of soldiers who had been following the bandits arrived at Sarsen's. They saw the bandits' horses tied to the hitching rail and got ready to attack. The house seemed dead quiet, without a single living soul inside.

"What's going on there?" a soldier asked, pointing at the chimney.

Another soldier moved closer to the chimney and shouted, "It's a man, no, a boy."

Yes, it was Zhanat. He was up to his armpits in the chimney; his face shone yellow in the sun, and his hair and eyelashes were glued with frost. Sarsen was lying near the doorstep, covered in blood. The door had a big lock on it.

They opened the lock and entered the house. Everything was scattered. The bandits were lying on the floor, dead. Bisara, also dead, was crouched in a corner. It became clear that the boy had used his body to close off the flue, and charcoal fumes had poisoned them all.

Sarsen, Zhanat, and Bisara were taken to the district center and buried there. The group commander made a speech; the soldiers saluted and shot their rifles into the air.

Someone set Sarsen's house on fire. They said it was Kozhakhmet, Bisara's father, who thought that the bandits should have no place in the ground. But there were no witnesses, and that case remained unsolved.

"That is the story of that place," said the old man, growing quiet.

Reflections

The old man called those years "The story of the life and death of a simple man." The talkative Sagdat fell silent; we stayed quiet as well. We did not talk, because there was nothing we could do to help Sarsen, Zhanat, and Bisara. We could not save them.

It amazes me how often powerlessness is a subject in our conversations. When you can only listen to what has happened, when you know everything and understand it, but cannot change it, that is also powerlessness.

****

Socialism's prime was in the postwar years. As Eastern European nations tried to recover, the Socialist regime was established, certainly not without participation of world Communist and proletarian movements, or the Soviets' mass ideological attack, or their military strength.

In a short amount of time, the following countries were added to the Socialist camp: the People's Republic of Poland and the Socialist Federal Republic of Yugoslavia in 1945; the People's Socialist Republic of Albania and the People's Republic of Bulgaria in 1946; the Socialist Republic of Romania in 1947; Czechoslovakia and the Democratic People's Republic of Korea in 1948; the People's Republic of Hungary, the German Democratic Republic, and the People's Republic of China in 1949; the Socialist Republic of Vietnam in 1954; the Republic of Cuba in 1959; and the People's Democratic Republic of Laos in 1975.

However, signs of its decay appeared in the first years of its creation. Disturbances in Hungary in 1956 were the first evidence for the collapse of the Socialist camp. They were followed by the riots of 1961 in Germany, the January Rebellion of 1963–1964 in Poland, and the Prague Spring from January 5 until August 20, 1968.

It is possible to say that Socialism appeared unexpectedly, with no prior foundations, in countries such as Poland, Yugoslavia, Albania, Bulgaria, Romania, Czechoslovakia, Hungary, and East Germany. Perhaps, that is why Socialism in those countries was blown away by the same unexpected wind that had brought it.

Socialism existed for 44 years in Poland (1945–1989), 47 years in Yugoslavia (1945–1992), 46 years in Albania (1946–1992), 44 years in Bulgaria (1946–1990), 42 years in Romania (1947–1989), 41 years in

Czechoslovakia (1948–1989), 40 years in Hungary (1949–1989), and 41 years in East Germany (1949–1990).

In the Mongolian People's Republic, Socialism lasted 68 years (1924–1992), and it lasted 17 years in the People's Democratic Republic of Laos (1975–1992). Thus, by 1992, the Socialist camp ceased to exist. Of the places in which Socialism ended, it lasted the longest—69 years (1922–1991)—in the USSR.

However, it has reigned in China for 61 years, from 1949 to the present day; time will show what will happen there next. I have my personal doubts about the viability and survivability of Socialism. It would be an exaggeration to say that Socialism has shown its worth in Cuba (since 1959) or in the People's Democratic Republic of Korea; besides, its future in these countries is rather illusive.

We should give prominence to the topic of Socialism in China. Russia, the motherland of Socialism, lost its status as a Socialist republic a long time ago and has taken a different path. However, China has maintained its Socialist ideas. It has also taken a leading position in the environment of the new market mechanism. This fact demands proper analysis and careful attention.

Deng Xiaoping's policy, "One country, two systems," proved to be efficient. It lifted China to a new level of development. Instead of denying the rationality of this theory, we should take a closer look at the situation and try to understand this phenomenon. To do so, we need to consider the unique Chinese mindset. What China has successfully developed may not be completely acceptable in other countries. Perhaps, we should talk of some of its elements or some specific method. The teaching of "One country, two systems" in present-day China has brought noticeable results. The combination of Socialism and market relations turned out to be favorable; it is an extraordinary social, economic, and political experience.

I presume that the key for this phenomenon not only lies in Socialism and capitalism, but also in peculiarities of the traditional essence of the Chinese nation. The Chinese strictly follow all traditions and rituals. The thinkers, politicians, and scientists seem to have removed, long ago, the principles and paradigms of orthodox Socialism, maintaining only the main principles of Socialism in politics. Indeed, they go beyond just maintaining them, but rely on them in everything.

One such principle is that the Communist Party acts as the authority for control and discipline. However, I also believe that the mindset of the Chinese never parted with Confucianism. The values of Socialism and capitalism act within the limits of the value system of Confucius.

The teaching of Confucius is comprehensible and familiar to everyone because it is a system of knowledge about humans and human values. The main categories of this system are father, son, duty, power, teacher, student, knowledge, and education. In the Kazakh culture, the philosophy of the late nineteenth-century sage Abai includes the very same value system. However, Abai has not yet become a Confucius for his nation because some Kazakhs prefer to search for cult figures in foreign countries rather than in their homeland. Our people really like to imitate, and this habit originates from a destructive negligent attitude toward their own national values.

I believe it will soon pass, and the situation will ultimately change for the better. The Chinese, however, take zealous pride in their values. They protect them, respect them, and celebrate them. Perhaps this commitment to their traditions is the key to their nation's global success.

****

Let us get back to Socialism in Kazakhstan. I developed a remonstrative attitude against it in the 1980s. I was certain that Socialism was a mistake in the history of humankind, from both theoretical and practical points of view.

The uprising of the Kazakhs against Soviet rule in December 1986 solidified all doubts about Socialism. All i's were dotted and all t's were crossed. It became obvious that new changes were bound to happen, that a new era was coming. Faith in Communism was exhausted. Liberal reforms began to be put in place. A spiritual restoration of the past commenced, bringing up new names, new facts that had been carefully hidden and guarded by censorship. A Russian, Gennady Kolbin, was appointed head of the Kazakh Communist Party, resulting in the December riots. He soon quit and was replaced by Nursultan Nazarbayev, who was an established political leader by that time, with good standing in the Kazakh Republic and abroad.

Those were our nation's first steps into the New Era, into the New Times of Independence. Soon disturbances in Russia and criticisms of Communist Party leaders resulted in the election of Gorbachev, the General Secretary of the Communist Party of the Union, as the first president of the USSR, during the Third Congress of People's Deputies in 1990. I do not know what Gorbachev was

A bronze relief in Independence Square, Almaty, Kazakhstan commemorating the December 1986 Kazakh Uprising against the appointment of a Russian (Gennady Kolbin) as head of state for the Kazakh SSR. The banner overhead reads: "For every people their own prince," meaning in this case one who is Kazakh. Photo © 2004 - R. Charles Weller.

thinking, but he put the matter of presidential elections in all fifteen union republics on the agenda.

That was the beginning of the collapse of Socialism. The ideas of proletarian dictatorship and the one-party system were renounced. In his interview with foreign journalists, Gorbachev declared, "We are one civilization." He aspired to combine a civilized environment with Socialism. But was it really possible?

Gorbachev started an active campaign to create the Commonwealth of Independent States. The Communists opposed it, and on August 19, 1991, a gang of eight men, headed by Gennady Yanayev, attempted a coup and forced Gorbachev to resign as President. It was a political phenomenon. Conservative-minded, left-wing forces tried to return to Socialism.

The newly elected President of Russia, Boris Yeltsin, strictly and courageously persisted in his civic duties under such circumstances. He signed a temporary truce with Gorbachev, claiming that, because Gorbachev was elected by the People's Deputies, the State Committee on the State of Emergency officials (the gang of eight) had broken the law when they forced him to resign the presidency.

Yeltsin freed Gorbachev, who was in custody in Foros, and thus he restored justice and lawfulness. However, Yeltsin did not stop there. On August 23, 1991, he invited Gorbachev to the deputies' session and, in his presence, he signed a decree of illegitimacy against the Communist Party. It was the political downfall of Socialism.

The Communist Party became a thing of the past. The nations went on to live without Marxist-Leninist ideology.

Soon the leaders of Russia, Ukraine, and Belarus finalized the fate of the USSR. On December 8, 1991, in the Belovezhskaya Pushcha Natural Reserve, they signed the Agreement Establishing the Commonwealth of Independent States.

Socialism existed 51 years in Estonia (August, 6, 1940, to August 20, 1991), 50 years in Lithuania (August 3, 1940, to March 3, 1990), 69 years in Georgia (December 30, 1922, to April 9, 1991), 69 years in the Russian Federation (December 30, 1922, to December 26, 1991), 51 years in Moldova (August 2, 1940, to June 23, 1991), 69 years in Ukraine (December 30, 1922, to August 24, 1991), 69 years in Belarus (December 30, 1922, to September 23, 1991), 62 years in Tajikistan (December 5, 1929, to August 31, 1991), 55 years in Kazakhstan (December 5, 1936, to December 16, 1991), 66 years in Uzbekistan (May 13, 1925, to August 31, 1991), and 69 years in Azerbaijan (December 30, 1922, to August 30, 1991).

Thus, the Union of Soviet Socialist Republics disappeared from the world map in December 1991.

CHAPTER 4
WHAT DID SOCIALISM GIVE TO KAZAKHS?

Socialism was introduced to the Kazakh land by force. Even though there was a division between wealthy and poor Kazakhs, there were no class differences. Wealth and poverty were associated with entrepreneurship or laziness, frugality or wastefulness. Abai called wastefulness the number one enemy of humanity. Wealth does not fall from the sky. It may come in two ways: the first way is through inheritance; the second way is through your own hard work. It often happens that some cannot preserve their inheritance from ancestors, but others may multiply theirs and become even wealthier. Active, sharp, and smart people can make a fortune in a short time; there is much proof of that in the history of humankind.

Mahmud Kashgari, a scholar who wrote a Turkic dictionary in the eleventh century, recorded a Turkic saying: "In forty years a poor man can become a wealthy man, and a wealthy man can become poor." It is the wisdom of our ancestors. Socialism destroyed that tradition by stating that all people had to be equal. In reality, its policy was aimed at making everyone poor. The establishment of universal equality sounds well intentioned, but it was not.

It seemed fair to take all the wealth from the rich people and divide it equally between everyone, but in reality that is called robbery. When all of a man's possessions are taken away from him in broad daylight, under the cover of revolutionary slogans, it is theft and violence; it is an abuse of human rights.

However, Bolsheviks felt that they had a right to act in such a manner. They justified their actions through the laws of class struggle, which they organized into an entire philosophy.

Kazakh society knew no classes or class struggle. Unfortunately, we did not even have a chance to contemplate and comprehend who we were and what society we lived in. Others did that for us. They also defined where and how we were supposed to proceed. According to them, Kazakhs lived in a feudal patriarchal system, which implied a class-based society, until the 1917 October Revolution.

In their view, the Kazakh society consisted of opposing parties, each with their own interests. One class was the ruling feudal lords, the expropriators; the other class was the oppressed poor people. The class struggle meant that both classes constantly fought each other, shedding blood in attempts to protect their interests. Soviet scholars arranged history along this vector and, therefore, regarded the liberation movements of Syrym Datov (1783–1797) and Isatay and Makhambet (1836–1838) as mutinies and rebellions of the poor.

So did feudalism really exist in Kazakhstan?

If it did, that meant Syrym Datov had fought for fourteen years, not against colonialists, but against Kazakh feudal lords. Thus, Bolsheviks were freeing poor people from feudal oppression and degraded villages when they instituted collectivization and established Socialism. However, if feudalism did not exist, then Datov had not fought against feudal lords; he had opposed the colonization of Kazakh society. Thus, Bolsheviks' claims that they had freed the nation from bloodsucking exploiters were false, and the collectivization carried out in Kazakhstan was an antinational policy. Socialism was not bringing liberation or equality to the nation; it was bringing a new form of enslavement.

There are two opposite points of view: Which of them is more credible? Which of them should we accept? Let us say, we agree with the first statement, that feudalism did exist in Kazakhstan; we admit that there was a class of feudal oppressors of the nation. What then is a feudal lord?

To be a feudal lord, one had to be a private owner of land, which had to be legally documented, with a seal, and passed on from generation to generation. Feudal lords keep workers and use poor people for labor. They traditionally constitute a social class.

Did the wealthy ('bai') among the Kazakh fit this definition? In their treatment of the epic novel *The Path of Abai*, by Mukhtar Auezov, school textbooks usually say that Abai Kunanbai was a feudal lord. Thus we have developed the strong impression that a wealthy peasant or herdsman is a feudal lord, and a feudal lord is a wealthy landowner. It may seem so at first. On the surface, a wealthy peasant or herdsman and feudal lord are similar. At some point in history, so-called scientists of the day could not distinguish copper from gold either; they mystified people with their alchemy, claiming that they could create gold out of copper.

In the beginning of the twentieth century, some peculiar historical alchemy united the concepts of feudal lord and wealthy peasant or herdsman into one idea, based on Marxist-Leninist teachings. These teachings found a home in Kazakhstan as well; they entered the minds of people and became their faith. It was a certain type of alchemy, which became a common perception. Alchemy, which had been chased out of natural science textbooks, had somehow made itself a solid and safe nest in the social sciences.

I previously mentioned the definition of a feudal lord. Let me now define a 'bai' (wealthy landowner).

1. The first occurrence of 'bai' was in the song of Kul Tigin (seventh–eighth century), and it had the same meaning then as it has now. Therefore, the word 'bai' has an ancient history. The song of Kul Tigin contains the lines: "I made the poor wealthy, I made a small nation numerous." 'Bai' was the name for a noble man, a benefactor. Kazakhs considered not only money and livestock but also human souls as wealth. This tradition is imbedded in the psychology of the people, in their customs and ways of life. That is why, whenever people greet each other, they ask about the well-being of both livestock and living souls.

2. Kazakhs did not have private property. It was a foreign notion to them. One can find sufficient proof of that in folk sayings and proverbs: "If you want to drink dregs, do it with everyone," "To share everything together with your relatives is a great celebration." These gems of folk wisdom were created through ideas of communal property. The history of communal property is many centuries long. It was based on extended transformation as the form of ownership that best matched the lifestyle of the nation. A wealthy owner of goods and property was an organizing and leading basis of that form.

3. It was indeed due to communal property that Kazakhs maintained their borders until the October Revolution. We had many enemies who wanted our land. Our ancestors, who defended it with deadly force, did not understand the idea of private property. A warrior hero (batyr) did not have it, and neither did a clan leader who spoke for the nation. Their main goal was to protect our borders. A wealthy landowner, in modern terms, was their sponsor.

In other words, wealthy peasants or herdsmen farmed, warriors protected the land, clan leaders led the nation. Since the land was common, there was common understanding of the need to protect the land and preserve its integrity.

Kazakhs have very close family ties with each other. The wealth of one person belongs to the other. That understanding was based on the perception of a common ancestral land (atameken). Wealthy peasants or herdsmen regulated this way of life, built on the idea of common property, which was the driving force of the society.

4. Since 'bai' corresponds to the notion of communal property, it cannot be analyzed separately from the village, which is a form of life organized around communal property. These concepts – wealthy peasant or herdsman and village – are two sides of the same coin. A village cannot exist without a wealthy landowner, just as a wealthy peasant or herdsman cannot exist without a village.

A village is not only a living space for the Kazakh, it is the form of their existence. Certainly, there were vile 'Karynbais' and stingy 'Shygaibais' among the wealthy peasants or herdsmen. But I am talking about general notions, not detailed variations. The modern word businessman provides the best analogy for the notion of 'bai'. A businessman is someone who can make a profit off some undertaking. A 'bai's' task was to benefit the village.

5. The concept of 'bai' is multidimensional; it suggests a business-like manner, an entrepreneurial spirit, proactiveness, and gumption. That may be the reason why the Kazakh name their babies Zhumabai, Maldybai, Aytabai, and so on.[19] The tradition to give such names is not accidental. Bai denotes professionalism or excellence; it is a synonym for a person of business acumen or success. Teaching a child to strive for wealth, culturally and spiritually as well as materially, is one of the lines of folk education.

To complete the political portrait of a 'bai', let me refer to the idea that is instilled in Kazakh children as an indisputable truth. Ever

---

[19] EN: Central Asians, including Kazakhs, name their children according to the meaning of the name, not after the parents or others. 'Zhumabai' means 'Rich in (the spirit of) Friday', i.e. rich in religious devotion, since Friday is the Muslim holy day; 'Maldybai' means 'Rich in Livestock'; and 'Aytabai' means 'Rich in Speaking' (cf. the English idea of 'Golden Mouthed').

since I was a child, I have heard the words "bai," "enemy of the people," "villain," "idler," and "lazybones" always connected together. My grandpa used to pick up breadcrumbs and hand them to me, "Eat up so you'll become a 'bai'." Teachers described wealthy peasants or herdsmen as evil enemies of the people, but Grandpa seemed to want me to become one. Later I discovered the reasons for such contradiction between these adults. In fact, it turned out that it was not so bad and shameful to be a wealthy landowner, but the mind of the nation remained clouded with seventy years of Bolshevik propaganda.

A wealthy peasant or herdsman is a person of risk. As the saying goes, "One bullet for the warrior, one string for the wealthy possessor of goods." The wealth of a wealthy is his livestock. He is surrounded with perils and misfortunes. He has no gold reserves or palaces or castles. His main capital, his revolving capital, is in his livestock.

There were few extremely wealthy people in the nation. A 'wealthy' person was a peasant of medium wealth, or middle class in modern terminology; it was impossible to accumulate great wealth in a small Kazakh village. A 'bai' intentionally limited his fortunes. This was a peculiarity of communal property. Another difference between a 'bai' and a feudal lord was that a 'bai' did not pass his wealth on to his descendants. While alive, he would allocate part of his possessions to his children, thus separating them from himself. After the separation, the children maintained their own households and did not depend on their father. Thus, after the death of a 'bai', there would be no scandals or fighting over an inheritance. The father's home traditionally went to the youngest son.

A Kazakh village knew no exploitation, but that did not mean there were no arguments, conflicts, or social injustices in Kazakh society. Social inequality (which is the basis for injustice) is a phenomenon that has been around for a long time. However, it does not pertain to class oppression only. There is inequality in Kazakh society, but it is not related to class exploitation. If we analyze the nature of inequality and its origins, we should recognize its ties with the human spirit and nature. Each person has his or her own individuality, his or her own intrinsic features.

The features, skills, and attributes of human nature are gifts from God. These properties are formed and developed throughout life and are revealed through one's humaneness, responsibility, and professional manner. For instance, some may have an inborn gift for drawing, writing poetry, singing, technology, or so on. One may see him- or herself as a ruler, a judge, or a manager, and strive to make that dream come true. Another person may be content and satisfied with a calm, unchanging life. Someone may dream of a full successful life, but do nothing to achieve it. Skills help a person find social independence. That is, one becomes a person of wealth; another becomes poor. Some want to be in the lead, while others want to be led. In order to avoid aggravating the situation between the poor and the wealthy, there was a whole system of village aqsaqals ('white beards', elders) and beys (clan leaders), who controlled order and balance.

Now let us turn our attention to social inequality in villages that had a 'bai', a peasant of average wealth, and a hired worker. We have already talked about the 'bai'. A peasant of average wealth is someone who had livestock; therefore he had enough for clothing and food. A poor man had very little livestock, maybe two or three horses, one or two cows, about ten sheep or goats. In general, a poor man sold his labor, his skills; for instance, he may have been a carpenter or a jeweler, or may have acted a courier or helped around the house. However, by working for hire, he could accumulate some wealth. Then there were also the poorest of the poor. Those were the idlers, who squandered their father's possessions and did not acquire any of their own. That was the entire population of an village. Certainly, a wealthy peasant or herdsman could benefit from hiring the poor.

There are two novels that show unique renditions of exploitation. The first is *Germinal*, by Emile Zola. This novel depicts the hard life of workers. A worker's family is starving. The wife goes to a bakery and asks for some bread in exchange for herself, but the baker demands the daughter instead. The poor woman agrees in despair. Such incidents certainly could not happen in a Kazakh village. Relatives may quarrel, but they would not stoop to murder or treachery. In peaceful days, no one starved in the village; everyone could rely on receiving help when needed. Exploitation like that in Western Europe simply did not exist.

The second novel that shows a version of class struggle and exploitation is *The Mother*, by Maxim Gorky. In this novel, Pavel is a regular worker, who drinks and parties like everyone else. In a Kazakh village, however, such behavior would be subject to severe reproof.

Reflections

The word 'adep'—politeness, decency, courtesy—has been engraved in my mind since childhood. Phrases like "polite child," "courteous daughter-in-law," "to observe the decencies," as well as many others like them could be heard regularly in every home.

What is meant by discourtesy, indecency, impoliteness? What was the value of those words? What did it mean to break customs, which were not punishable by law?

When I asked the elderly Beysen those questions, he replied, "Son, the very word 'adep' is so worn out nowadays, it has lost any meaning, never mind the customs. A daughter-in-law in olden times would not dare to say the name of her father-in-law or brother-in-law out loud, so she would give them a nickname, for example, White Beard or Big Heart. That was the tradition of courtesy, but what is left today of that tradition?"

"Aqsaqal, the times are changing; nothing is eternal in this world. New people come to the world and bring something new with them."

"I do not mind; the world is certainly changeable. Clothes wear out, views change. But courtesy and respectfulness are equally necessary for people in all times. That is all I am saying."

I agreed with the words of the old man. Indeed, human nature remains unchanged in all ages and eras.

However, as new times come, we gain something, but we also lose something irretrievably. How do we define the line between what can be lost and what should be fought for? What new things are acceptable, and what should we avoid like the plague?

I contemplated these questions for a long time, but could not come to a full understanding, so I addressed the old man again, "Aqsaqal, tell me, how did people honor traditions? What force made people observe them?"

The old man grew quiet and then said, "All right, but it will be a tragic story. To be honest, people broke traditions in the old days too."

The old man paused, looked at me searchingly, as if doubting whether to tell me or not. Then he asked, "Do you have any traditions and customs now, or did you just hear those words from someone?"

"We have Communist morality. We have classroom activities on the topic of morality at school." But I could tell that the old man did not understand.

"Does that mean that your current 'adep' is the behavior and habits of present day Communists?"

"Yes, aqsaqal, Communists are true adherents of Soviet morality, and they serve as an example for everyone."

"Oh, son, maybe in other lands there are people such as you describe, but among those that I know, none can be considered an observer of 'adep'."

I started to think about the village's Communists. The head of our farm was a Communist, and he could down two liters of vodka in one sitting. And when he got drunk, the obscenities just poured out of him.

Our school principal was a Communist. He lived with an unmarried woman, Mayra; they said he was divorcing his wife. So, who else? Right, the veterinary assistant, Asanali, he was also a Communist, but he was about to be tried for confusing the state budget for his own.

The old man was right; we had no exemplary Communist in our kolkhoz. Wait a minute. What about Zhomart, the teacher? He was a real man. Oh, but he was not a Communist. Last week, the head of the farm had gotten drunk during Kauken's daughter's wedding and had attacked Zhomart with his fists yelling, "I am telling you nicely—get out of my way. Do not pester me, Communist, or you'll regret it." That was the situation in our village.

As for me, I was a student at a teachers college, who needed to write a term paper on the subject of 'adep'. Where else could I look, if not to the old people?

So I kept on questioning the elderly Beysen, trying to fish for necessary information. The aqsaqal had seen the beginnings of the kolkhoz; he was a war veteran and a father of eight children. It was a pity that he was not a Communist, but despite that, it seemed that he could tell me about 'adep'.

I sat closer to the old man and tried to persuade him, "Aqsaqal, help me. I am collecting information about the past."

"Oh, I don't know if my story will be good for your paper, but since you are asking, let it be so. My father told me this story. It is about traditions and customs." The old man paused, and then began.

The Elderly Beysen's Story

Bogembai, the warrior, was nearing fifty and did not go off to battle very often anymore. He could not really be called old yet, but his moustache and beard were touched with grey. Even so, he still held the same status in the village.

One year, a problem erupted. It was spring. People were getting ready to leave for the summer pastures, so everyone was in a happy mood. The young people were especially excited, anticipating secret dates, festive games, and relaxing times. It was an unwritten law of the steppe, a habit deep-seated in the minds of steppe people.

The beautiful Gulsum, the young wife of Serikpai, had just recently moved in to his house. She was only seventeen, and she seemed discontented with his affections. It also made her angry when her husband, who thought he was superior to everyone, would grow quiet and meek at the very name of Bogembai. However, when she saw Bogembai for herself, she was lost, lovesick.

Gulsum was confident of her charms, and she decided to conquer the brave Bogembai. No matter how hard she tried, though, Bogembai would not accept her advances. Gulsum bit her lips in disappointment, and angrily ground her teeth at her powerlessness. It did not improve her mood when she noticed Bogembai looking at her with obvious aversion.

Gulsum nurtured her resentment, "You just wait; I'll get even with you," she thought, as her eyes met those of the imperturbable and passionless Bogembai.

Finally, the day came when she could publicly snub the man who had rejected her flirtations.

Bogembai was not actually immune to Gulsum's affections. But the more he thought about her, the more she inspired some instinctive worry in him; a soul-chilling fear embraced his heart at the sight of her beauty.

He could not share his worries with anyone. Perhaps Analyk, mother of Serikpai and wife of the village's older brother, would understand, but he felt uneasy going to her. It did not befit a man to meddle in her affairs.

Since her husband had died, she had become the mother of the village, and no one dared to contradict her. Her name had been given to her out of deep respect and admiration for her strong and virile character. She had two sons; the younger one, Sarybai, had also gotten married recently and lived in a separate yurt.

Analyk was also worried and wanted to share her concerns with Bogembai. Since Gulsum had come to their house, her son, who had been courteous and polite before, had changed; he committed actions unworthy of a man. When alone, she thought long about the problem.

Her son was in a position that put him above Bogembai, even though he was younger than the warrior. Regardless, he would never think to compete with the warrior or, especially, show him any disrespect. That would be a grave violation of the centuries-old order and eternal traditions. If such a thing happened, a great disaster would occur. The nation that lost its traditions, would lose its power.

Her father had said, "My daughter, it is not easy to rule the village-nation; one needs great power, a clear mind, and fine reckoning. Bogembai will live among you, but remember, a warrior should be given a place of honor. The power of the village-nation is in the incontestable authority of Bogembai. As leader, you must ensure that people's faith in him stays strong so that they always show him honor and respect. If you break this tradition, there will be great trouble."

"Ata, the world consists of opposites. Each thing has its pair: man and woman, good and evil, decency and indecency," Analyk had started to say.

The old man had interrupted her, "My daughter, what you say is only true at first glance. In reality, a man and a woman make a pair only if their souls are congenial, if a woman can genuinely respect her husband. Good and evil may be in harmony only if there is some good in the evil, and some evil in the good; what was good gradually turns into what is evil, and what was evil turns into what is good. Courtesy and rudeness do not go together. Rudeness is the result of a poorly developed mind, whereas courtesy comes from the union of the mind and the heart."

So Analyk felt trouble coming, but she could not explain it to anyone. She was scared of her son's rapid changes and of her daughter-in-law's insatiable lust for life. They say that such people have a short life. Once, she had almost talked to Bogembai about it, but she had changed her mind when she realized she could not properly explain her suspicions to him. If she could not explain, then why should she bother the warrior with trifles?

"It probably comes from my old age," she decided and sent a prayer to the Almighty, asking for his grace and mercy. She thought of her father again. He had said that there was only one way to fight an insatiable lust for life. You must remember that you are a guest on this earth and thank God, day and night, for giving life to you.

Analyk cheered up. She knew what she had to do. When they went to the pastures, she would send her son away from the house and have a talk with her daughter-in-law.

However, man proposes, but God disposes. Nomadism was not easy; migrations required many days of preparation. By tradition, the caravan was led by a man who could repel an enemy attack, if necessary. For Analyk's village-nation, the caravan would be headed by Bogembai. It was tradition, and it did not occur to anyone to change that order. Analyk approved. Even though she was the elder of the tribe, she was only a woman, and tradition said it was the destiny of a man to protect the lives of the people.

Before setting off, it was customary for the caravan leader to ask for a blessing from the village mother. Only after the blessing ritual, could they begin the journey. God forbid if someone broke the established custom. It was a severe offence, and a severe punishment awaited the wrongdoer.

It had been one day since Bogembai had set off. The rest were getting ready for departure, packing their things onto the wagons, organizing the livestock into herds. Everyone was divided into groups, waiting for their turn to receive blessings for their travel. The caravan was stretched out, with groups leaving hours or days apart, so that the animals could be grazed along the way and there would be room to set up camps at night.

Suddenly, talk started going around.

"Have you heard about that shame? What should we do now? Who do we follow?"

"I would never have imagined that something like this could happen."

"It is that bitch, Gulsum. It must have been her idea," the old men of the village said.

The younger men sat on the top of a hill to take council.

"Bogembai must indeed be growing old. Nobody would have dared think of doing something like this before."

"Serikpai has broken ancestral traditions. Trouble is sure to follow."

"All right, there's no use sitting here talking about it. Let's find a solution."

"We'll send a message to Bogembai."

"We should send messengers to Analyk as well; she must have heard the rumors by now."

"So be it. We'll send Sarybai and Serkebai to our village mother."

Sarybai and Serikpai were brothers and also good friends. Sarybai always deferred to Serikpai in everything. Though Sarybai had great prestige in his own right, he respected Serikpai's seniority. But despite his youth, Sarybai was brave and courageous; he had the character of a warrior.

Serikpai had disgraced Bogembai by committing an unheard of deed. He had migrated on his own, gone a different direction, disregarding everyone.

Sarybai's heart roiled with rage. He was angry with Serikpai—That idiot!—for losing his reason to that slutty Gulsum.

It was obvious she had beguiled him into doing this egregious thing. But the man would have to be held accountable. It was unlikely that Serikpai would agree to come back easily. He was not a child; he knew what he was doing. It might result in bloodshed, and that was the most dreadful thing.

Sarybai and Serkebai told Analyk about everything.

She replied immediately, "Even though he is my son, I cannot forgive him this insult to Bogembai. Go and punish him as necessary."

"Serikpai knew it was a grave sin. He is probably prepared for anything," Sarybai said.

"Do what you must. Destroy the enemy that we have raised. Our ancestors' spirits will not forgive us if we do not avenge Bogembai's honor," so Analyk gave them her blessing.

She saw how difficult this was for Sarybai, who realized he would have to lay hands on his own brother. "Do your duty alone; do not involve anyone else."

When Sarybai and Serkebai arrived at Serikpai's wandering village, Gulsum swept out of the yurt, smiled coyly, and said, "Dismount your horses, my brothers-in-law. Feast on whatever God has sent us."

Sarybai felt attracted to her and got angry at himself. "Yes, a vixen like that can make anyone lose his head," he thought. He rode over to Gulsum and lifted her up. With a swift sweep of his knife, he cut off her braids and then threw Gulsum aside. He hung her braids on one of the yurt's poles.

Then he and Serkebai rode a safe distance away from the village. Serkebai was still hoping that Serikpai would realize his mistake so this could end peacefully. Maybe even Gulsum would come to her senses.

However, Sarybai, red with anger, was about to explode. "I know my brother. When he gets angry, he has no mercy for anyone. If he gets on his war horse, especially with his spear, no amount of talking will help, nothing will stop him."

"He broke his oath. Any weapon in the hands of an oath breaker has no force," replied Serkebai.

Soon they saw Serikpai riding toward them in a cloud of dust, his spear at the ready. Immediately, they both jumped on their horses and reached for their arrow quivers.

"Wait, Serikpai, let's talk about this," Sarybai shouted, but Serikpai did not listen and launched his spear at them.

They dodged the spear, braced their bows, and let their arrows fly. Both arrows hit their target. Serikpai bent over, grabbing his horse's mane, and slowly slipped to the ground.

The men grabbed the horse. They threw Serikpai's body across its back, and seated Gulsum on it, facing its tail. Then they led the horse to Bogembai.

When Bogembai learned of what had happened, he sighed heavily, "You shouldn't have been so hasty. He was my faithful companion. He came to my rescue many times in battles. His gullibility must have led him astray. You should have warned me."

Consoling the warrior, Analyk said, "He observe proper manners ('adep'), Bogembai, and that is a contagious disease. Customs and traditions are the forces that unite people. We have to do everything we can to make sure the people stay together."

The old man stopped talking and started to stroke his beard with his thin fingers, agitated as much as I was by his story. His thoughts were still with the fallen Serikpai. Or maybe he was thinking of the grieving Bogembai, or of the mother who had shed many bitter tears in sadness for her son but, despite everything, had remained strong in spirit and faithful to the customs. Perhaps, the old man was scolding himself for telling such an intimate story to a raw youth who might not even understand it fully.

The old man sat deep in thought for a long time, remembering the past. Then his wife's voice rang out, "Old man, the tea is ready."

"Well, let's go to the table," the aqsaqal said, getting up with a groan.

I thought of the face of the farm head, red from vodka, as he had pounced on the teacher. "Poor Analyk, God bless your motherly heart," I thought, and followed the aqsaqal.

Reflections

It is true that wealthy herdsmen were against universal collectivization. The rightness of their position has been confirmed by the present-day reality. It was a mistake to impose universal collectivization on the village ('aul') system, which had been established over the centuries, and to subject Kazakhs to complete Sovietization. The liquidation of wealthy herdsmen as a class in 1928 led to the tragic events of the 1930s, to the ruin and starvation of the Kazakhs in the Great Famine. Bolsheviks hid behind the necessity of class struggle, which had never existed in Kazakh society. They destroyed peaceful villages and chased Kazakhs away in all directions. Those who opposed them were crushed as Basmachi bandits or as nationalists. The surviving intellectuals who believed in the Bolsheviks' slogans to fight the nonexistent feudalism, actively swung into action. Why did it happen that way?

The Kazakh who led a clan-based life had never seen or known class struggle. The social inequality that was intrinsic to a Kazakh village excluded the kinds of blunt opposition and cruelty inherent in class struggle. Minor troubles and conflicts that occurred between wealthy peasants or herdsmen and poor people were promptly settled by a council of aqsaqals and controlled by the middle generation. No matter what happened, the village life was autonomous, and village people preferred not to make unsettling events known to the public. At the same time, however, some intellectuals silently sided with Soviets and supported the ideas of Socialism.

That was their mistake. When the campaign to destroy wealthy peasants and herdsmen, as a class of exploiters, started in 1928, when plundered Kazakh villages grew empty, the intellectuals realized their mistake, although it was too late. At first glance, communal-tribal and collective-Socialist property seemed almost identical in their essence. Later, though, it became clear that they were as far apart from each other as heaven and earth. Communal-tribal property was much more complex and multidimensional.

In a village (i.e., in the case of communal-tribal property) there are two types of property. The first is the wealthy herdsman's livestock, the second is each household's livestock. A wealthy herdsman's livestock was considered common because the poor, the hired workers who worked for the wealthy herdsman, were paid for their labor with the very same livestock. This wealth was necessary for life; it was a type of income. If the wealthy herdsman had no livestock, people would have nowhere to work and make a living. People also had their own livestock, and everyone owned some part of that. Common livestock was the basis of life. That is why those who did not work harmed themselves. At essence, communal-tribal property is similar to a joint-stock company; it complies with the same principles.

Thus, I assert that Kazakh society did not have class exploitation. Therefore, there was no feudalism. What happened then? Who misled the people? Was it Marx or Lenin?

As for Marx, he is completely innocent here. He spent his life writing about methods of Asian production. In spite of this, a discussion flared up in Soviet society in the 1920s and 1930s regarding the economic formations of society. Eventually, the Soviet orientalist Vasily Struve (1889-1965) defined five formations: primitive-communal society, slave-owning system, feudalism, capitalism, and Communism (with Socialism as its first phase). His theory was based on the teachings of Karl Marx and Vladimir Lenin. The minds of millions of students and young generations were poisoned by deceitful assumptions. The theory of formations was so deep-rooted in our brains that even a slight doubt was seen as a crime.

There still may be some followers of the theory of five formations. Perhaps one should be familiar with them, but I do not want to argue about that here. I only want to say that this information was not necessary for Kazakh society. Marx wrote his reflections on the nations of Western Europe. He did not know the East, or Asia; he had never been here. Even when talking about Communism, he referred exclusively to Europe. If Marx's works and papers were absolutely necessary, it would have been more useful for us to know his conclusions on Asian methods of production. Unfortunately, our intellectuals could not think independently and only followed the designated path.

Our Europeanized intellectuals based their assertions on the teachings of Karl Marx and claimed that feudalism did exist in Kazakhstan; they even pointed out its unique patriarchal manifestation.

The core of the problem was in the differences between the West and the East. To be more precise, the nations of the West and the East differed in their production methods, worldviews, and specific perceptions of reality.

The allegation that Kazakhs lived in an era of patriarchal feudalism fit in well with Bolshevik ideology; otherwise, it would have been difficult for them. No classes would mean the absence of class struggle. Then the battle to protect an exploited working nation would have turned out to be a war against the nation itself. It would have been obvious.

In the early 1900s, Lenin entered a heated discussion with Marxist theoretician Georgi Plekhanov regarding feudalism. Plekhanov claimed that the Asian production method was predominant in Russia. Lenin, however, declared that ever since ancient times, feudal relations had been thriving in Russia.

Feudalism and Asian production methods were confused in Karl Marx's time as well. For instance, when Marx was making notes on English judge John Budd Phear's book *The Arya village in India and Ceylon*, he wrote, "That ass Phear described the organization of a village community as feudal."

Here we see that Marx strictly distinguished between a village community and a feudal community. Why then do we call life in a village community feudal? I believe that the Kazakh economic mode of life should be analyzed, not from the position of feudalism, but through the framework of the Asian method of production.

The Asian production method is not a fully elaborated concept in academics. It is not my task here to study it in-depth, with all its specifics and details. Instead, the goal is to understand the village method of production.

Based on the above, can we say that feudalism existed in Kazakhstan? Certainly we cannot. If the land was communal property, people were not divided into classes. If people formed groups within the society, in accordance with their generic characteristics, where could the feudal oppression come from? The theory of feudalism migrated to us from Europe. Kazakh society had no room for feudalism. A claim to the contrary would be due to ideological pressure. It would be a forced implantation of distorted and erroneous ideas. European and Russian measures are not suitable for Kazakhstan, which requires corresponding Kazakh measures. However, if we were to consider Kazakh measures, all questions regarding feudalism in Kazakhstan would be eliminated.

****

The Socialist regime came to power and destroyed the Kazakh way of life, which had been established through centuries but which was suddenly deemed patriarchal and stagnant. Socialist propagandists ensured that the idea that it was good to be a wealthy peasant or herdsman became seen as erroneous thinking of the past. To hire people and to provide them with shelter and food and a chance to earn their livings were machinations of evil parties and an exploitative class. The enemies had to be detected and destroyed, tried and exiled, hung or shot; their property had to be confiscated; the class enemy, the **kulaks**, had to be eliminated.

That was the course of "the small October" in Kazakhstan, the campaign of dekulakization was finished. Millions of people, in panic and chaos, abandoned their belongings and sought safety in other countries. Thus, the present-day problem of oralmans (returnees) originated in those years.[20]

During the first years of independence, I met a colonel who had served in Afghanistan before returning to his native land. According to him, it had been turbulent in Afghanistan for a long time. For about a hundred years the English ruled in Afghanistan, later the Americans came, and then the Soviets—Afghanistan was constantly being claimed by greedy hands. "For Afghans, to be at war is the same as to take a stroll in fresh air," Friedrich Engels once noted.

I suspect those words referred to the militant nature of the Afghan; I doubt that war could be a joy to anyone. War is a frightful madness. Leo Tolstoy gave it a deep and profound description in his novel **War and Peace**. Regardless, we

---

[20] EN: Kazakhs fled during this period, among other places, to China, Mongolia, Afghanistan, Iran, and Turkey.

need to acknowledge that Afghans have been in a constant state of war. It is a very unfortunate fate for a nation.

Over lunch, the colonel told us about Afghanistan, about his service there as a military adviser. He appeared to know the political situation in Afghanistan; he was well informed of social, political, and other standings. He spoke mainly Kazakh, but occasionally inserted Russian words. It was clear he was trying to conceal resentment and discontent.

I have heard and read a lot about Afghanistan to help clarify the situation. Some things were new to me, especially archival and documentary data. I listened to my companion attentively, trying not to miss anything.

The colonel had served abroad his entire military career, and had returned to his homeland only right before his retirement. From his words I understood that he had not yet outlived his communistic stereotypes.

For a long time, he spoke about those who ruled in Afghanistan and about American and Soviet policies. Suddenly, he stopped and said, "I will tell you about the time I met a Kazakh family in the Afghan land."

We were ready to listen.

The Colonel's Story

It was a mistake to bring troops to Afghanistan.[21] Before that, we, the officers, were in good standing with the locals; we served as military advisers. The authorities welcomed us as well. But everything changed after our soldiers arrived.

We sat quietly waiting for him to tell us about his meeting with the Kazakh family.

Back then, in Afghanistan, I was invited to the house of a Kazakh family. Fearing provocation, I first made some inquiries about the family—who they were, what they did.

When I went to see them, I brought weapons and two soldiers with me for protection. Their house was surrounded by a tall fence. I left one soldier in the car and took the other one with me. The host had set a table right in the yard. I noticed that he seemed to have two wives: one was sitting next to him, the other was serving tea. The host was a tall,

---

[21] EN: See esp. Gregory Fremont-Barnes, The Soviet–Afghan War 1979–89 (Osprey Publishing, 2012); The Russian General Staff, *The Soviet-Afghan War: How a Superpower Fought and Lost*, tr. and ed. Lester W. Grau and Michael A. Gress (University Press of Kansas, 2002).

red-bearded middle-aged man of few words. We had tea in silence. I noticed that the teacup was held together by thin wire. I was very surprised and remembered that I had seen that in our villages during the war. I thought that their life must not have been too good.

As if he had read my mind, the host said, "My situation has been lousy the whole time I have been living here."

I said, "If you are not doing very well in this country, what made you leave your homeland and settle here?"

The host looked at me sternly, "Who would abandon his homeland of his own volition, dear man? Your government destroyed so many worthy people."

I grew angry, "Could it be that you were among those who killed Bolsheviks and joined the Basmachi?"

He jerked up his head, raised his hand as if trying to rebut my words, "Dear man, my father and my grandfather were wealthy people. God gave us our wealth. My father had two wives and eight children. Their calm and happy life ended suddenly overnight. They wanted to confiscate our belongings; that's why we were forced to leave."

The second wife bowed and said courteously, "Help yourselves to some tea."

A weighty silence descended. I was confused, and strong feelings raged inside me. It was clear to me that this was an enemy of our people before me, a wealthy herdsman's son. "Look at him now," I thought. "He lives abroad and even has two wives."

The host broke the silence, "There is no way to hide from you Communists. We left our homeland, moved here, but you found your way here as well. Oh Allah, will there be a day when we are set free from you?"

I could not stand it any longer and radioed the soldier in the car to get ready. The soldier sitting next to me looked at me in bewilderment. I stood up, "Dear man, I thank you for the tea, but I cannot thank you for your courtesy." I headed for the door.

"They are always that way—straightforward, blunt, and never able to have a calm conversation," the host said to his wives loudly and defiantly, making sure I heard him.

I shook with fury, but then the Tajik soldier said in Russian, "Judging by how they greet their guests, they seem like nice people, don't they?"

I reflected on their chipped cups wrapped in wires and thought, "They are not good people, but lost ones." I sat quiet, not saying anything.

The colonel must have read something from my silence and continued, "Yes, if the old man had attempted to attack, we had enough weapons in the car to blow up his entire house."

I looked at the colonel and thought of the saying, "Crudeness is no goodness." Meanwhile, the colonel turned to his food, indicating that the conversation was over.

I felt an urge to step outside for some fresh air.

****

Socialism was implanted into Kazakh life by force, but at the same time, our Kazakh intellectuals took an active part in the revolution of 1917, which began the establishment of Socialism in Russia.

It seems to me that people who supported the idea of Socialism were wrong. They believed that Socialism was the way to free people of colonial dependency. Later they must have realized their error.

However, our spiritual leaders saw that they could not break Bolshevism. So even though they cooperated with the Bolsheviks, they did everything possible to make people's lives easier. It was a diplomatic approach that was justified by its good results. Our people received good training and education; national culture was on the rise, and science was thriving.

Thirdly, the reason for their misconception was that they tried to find Socialist ideas in the ways and lives of Kazakhs. But the Kazakhs were absolutely free of them. Perhaps some elements, parts of the whole, had some resemblance, but that was it.

There are many ideas about justice and fair societies in the literary, art, and spiritual treasuries of our nation. For instance, there is a village tradition to join together to see the deceased off on his or her final journey or to greet a new bride. Everything is done in the public eye and with public discussion. There is even a tradition to name a child Kuanysh (Joy). It happens in everyday life. Traditional folklore and art glorify and celebrate fairness and provide examples.

For instance, the well-known Turkic poet-sages Jirenshe Sheshen, Asan Kaigy, and others advocated fairness in building an affluent society. The successors of their dreams and aspirations were Bolsheviks, who hid behind the assurance that they were the government of the poor.

Thus, the words of the poor became synonymous with the ideas of Socialism. However, they were not the same. In a Kazakh village, a poor man could not help another poor man. He would get help from the patriots of his tribe—imams, wealthy peasants or herdsmen, clan leaders—because along with their wealth, they also possessed compassion. No matter what kind of a man the wealthy peasant or herdsman was, if he did not have compassion, he could never be respected in the society. There were almost no moneygrubbers or misers in Kazakh society.

Fourthly, people who were fanatically devoted to Bolshevism were called activists among the people. Those people inflicted irreparable damage on the nation. Activists, according to the scholar Akhmet Baitursynov, were the weeds who grew up in the village. They pitted people against each other, instilled fear and humbleness. They were rigorous guards of the Bolshevist policies. Unfortunately, they outgrew their small role as petty pests; they strengthened and formed a large army of national Communists.

Even though it is all in the past, we still have to admit it as a fact. In the simplest terms, we Communists propagated and preached the ideas of Bolshevism in Kazakhstan, thus misdirecting the nation. I am certainly nowhere near thinking that, under Socialism, people lived in total blindness, but it was true indeed that the minds of people were clouded; they lost their freedom and became slaves.

Regarding this matter, my position is similar to that of Friedrich August von Hayek, the author of The Road to Serfdom, *which is about Socialism.*

What can we say now if we once worked in Bolshevik organizations and called that service our business, called our servile mind our Communist thinking. Fathers and sons were set in opposition to each other, and that was called Communist morality. Therein lies our fault, the fault of Communists.

People sometimes have another name for fault: sinfulness. And that may be closer to the truth.

If we pause to think about it, we all spend our lives committing actions, making decisions, falling into sin. The saying goes, "When the angel sees gold, he wanders off from the path of righteousness." It is improbable that any mortal could live a life without sin. Is there really a path that can help us avoid it?

Christian and Muslim religions provide full and complete answers to that question. If you feel sinfulness in you, turn to the path of purification, and you will be forgiven by God and the people.

I want to tell a story that happened to my contemporaries.

My Story

Tursynbai, Bolat, and Mergen missed their classmate Khasenkhan. One day, in hopes of improving their health with the curative waters of Alakol Lake, they surprised him with a visit.

Khasenkhan, beside himself with joy, did not know where to seat his dear guests, how to offer them a better welcome. Questions and memories broke out: remember this... did you know that...

But Khasenkhan noticed that there was something strange going on between the friends. They would be talking about something and then suddenly start to argue, each trying to persuade the other, but they could not come to an agreement.

At first he did not pay attention to their quarrels, but gradually he was dragged into their discussions. The conversation lasted for two hours. So many countless words and innermost thoughts spilled from the depths of their hearts. The talk, which had started from a trifling remark, had turned into a debate.

Then Khasenkhan added fuel to the fire. Every now and then the guests would start talking about Stalin. Khasenkhan could not bear it anymore and blurted out, "Just let Stalin be. What is his guilt before you? If it were not for him, you all would be under the fascist heel now."

That was the way Khasenkhan was; he would stay quiet and then drop a bomb you could not have even dreamed of.

Tursynbai replied indignantly, "Does that mean you think everything we've been talking about is just hot air?"

Bolat chimed in disapprovingly, "The minds of many have not cleared yet. Everyone is still in the grip of old dogmas and past illusions."

"During the Great Chief's (Stalin) rule, thousands of people became victims of his despotism; they lost their homes, families, and friends. Hundreds of worthy and talented sons were shot. You can't ignore that, Khasenkhan," Mergen said.

Khasenkhan was silent, deep in thought, maybe searching for the right words. Or maybe he was trying to keep hold of feelings that were bubbling up on the inside. Finally, he noticed that his friends were watching him, waiting for an answer. He decided to change the topic. "All right, let's drop Stalin. Let others judge him. But is it really fair to single out our honored aqsaqals and authors of old textbooks and accuse them of every sin? Why can't they just be left alone to die with dignity?"

The room grew quiet.

With the advent of glasnost, the papers had been reporting unassailable evidence of the shady ventures some of our science and culture masters took part in during those well-remembered times. Everyone understood that it was much more difficult to accuse those still-living, respectable people, than to pick apart the rule of the long-deceased Stalin.

Tursynbai said, "That's just the way it was then. You couldn't swim against the tide."

"It was the work of individual people," Bolat added. "The cult of personality is not a trend in the age of developed Socialism."

"Let Socialism be," Mergen replied. "We didn't even get a taste of true Socialism. Sure, we had misconceptions; that's not the point. It's not about humanism in general, but about how one could survive in each particular situation and still maintain his good name."

"Humanism!" Bolat scoffed. "What humanism are you talking about? There were no morals then, only mere ideology. Not a single moral system in the world had what we had. The son of an 'enemy of the people' couldn't go to a Soviet school; he couldn't become a member of the Komsomol."

Tursynbai declared, "Morals come from the consciousness of the crowd. It's difficult to give a scientific definition to a collective consciousness or a crowds' interest."

"Universal human morals are above the consciousness of the crowd; they're higher than its interests. That is what we have missed in our times," Bolat said.

"Guys, stop evading the topic," Khasenkhan said. I'm waiting for your answer to my question."

"The answer is obvious," Bolat began. "We need to be brutally honest; we must call 'black' what is black, and 'white' what is white. Those responsible, surrounded by all kinds of honors and regalia, should be held accountable. While the executed were rotting beneath the sod, they sat safely in warm offices, praising the government and making their careers."

"Calm down, Bolat," Tursynbai said. "What about the humanism you talked about? I think it's unnecessary to judge those who could not resist and just drifted with the current. There is no need to stir up the past. They are people, too. They didn't do all that on purpose."

"Then what should we do about those who were accessories to the government, those who scribbled accusations and slanders instead of making at least some effort to stay quiet and not suck up to the regime?" Bolat asked.

"It's a complicated situation," Mergen replied. "You're talking about accusations, but what if they genuinely believed in what they wrote? One can be sincerely mistaken; faith can be blind, too."

"I think that the forum of conscience is the highest justice for them," Tursynbai put it. "Their penance will be accepted by the people. Remember how we believed Brezhnev? It wouldn't hurt us to repent and clear ourselves of yesterday's illusions as well."

"But," Bolat said, "villainy and cruelty may come back again if they're not rooted out. That's the real threat of our time. We want to know the truth so we can make sure that such evil doesn't happen again."

"I agree," Mergen said. "We dig to the roots for the sake of a happy tomorrow, to make sure the horror of those days never comes back. Historical consciousness is born in the same way as a baby comes to this world. A mother suffers through the pains of labor to bring a tiny life into this world. Similarly, history stays in the womb of its mother until the time is ripe. Then the day comes when Mother Time, in the throes of labor, bears her baby. A newborn needs care and attention; otherwise, the baby may not survive, like in the 1950s. Years go by, and now we are once again watching the great mother: When will the child be born?"

"I agree with you, Mergen," Bolat said. "But we should not shift the burden of our guilt to future generations. There is no guilt that cannot be forgiven. Then absolution and peace will come, but only if our hearts have not been hardened. The young ones watch us, puzzled: they were saying one thing yesterday and a different thing today, so where is the truth? That's why the older generation should test themselves and their hearts, whether they need penance and sincere repentance or not. The heart will not lie."

Tursynbai replied, "The sworn enemies of history are villainy and cruelty; its foundations are good deeds. Villainy is fleeting, good is constant."

"Villainy and cruelty are very shifty," Mergen said. "People commit them very skillfully. That's why it's sometimes very hard to find proof."

"All the secrets will come out sooner or later," Bolat said. "Villainy is created by cowardice, and cowardice is blind. Time passes and impudence emerges as clear as tracks in white snow."

"Good and the evil are inseparable," Khasenkhan explained. "If there were no evil, we could never distinguish the good. The very existence of evil is a historical principle and necessity. The history of humanity is the history of evil."

"But do we need to remember and stir up the past all the time, to bear anger and revenge inside? When do we do good then?" Tursynbai asked.

Bolat replied, "If you do not eradicate evil, it may take root."

"It's an eternal problem," Tursynbai said. "Let me tell you a Chechen parable about anger and revenge."

In ancient times, two friends set off on the road. On their way, they squabbled over something small. One thing led to another, and they ended up attacking each other with daggers. They fought long, and finally one of them mounted his horse and held his dagger to his opponent's heart. The defeated one begged for mercy, saying that he was the only son his father had, that he had never married, so he had no progeny. His friend cooled down immediately, blaming himself for his hot temper, for almost killing his friend in anger over something stupid. He helped his friend up, hugged him, and asked for forgiveness.

But his companion turned out to be a sly and lying coward, and he harbored enmity. He decided to take revenge no matter what.

Exhausted from the long fight, they decided to rest. They tied up their horses, put the saddles under their heads, and fell asleep.

The man who had won the argument was sleeping soundly, but the other man had anger roiling in his heart, and sleep eluded him. The trustful friend of the villain did not even have a chance to move before the dagger took its toll. As the man's soul slowly left its body, the villain calmly saddled his horse, watching with interest for his victim's last breath.

The dying man knew that his life was over, and there would be no one to bury him. His body would be left on the deserted steppe to be picked over by crows. With his last ounces of strength, he turned his head to the rich blooming flowers and meadow grass and whispered a plea, "Oh beauty and pride of our wide steppes, grass that has spread in a soft carpet ever since Adam and Eve came down to our sinful land. Oh flowers, watered by Eve's tears. I call to you with my last request. I will die now, but there is no one to tell my son, my heir, about my death. You are the only witnesses of the evil deed committed here. When my son has grown and passes through here, please stop him and tell him what happened. That is my request." Then he died.

"What nonsense. What can flowers and grass do?" the murderer laughed. He whipped his horse and rode off.

Many years passed. Once again, two people met in the steppe and became companions.

One of them was a young lad; the other was an elderly man. On their way, they talked of this and that, and when they grew tired, they decided to rest. The old man remembered the bloody incident from long ago as he sat and smirked at the exuberant vegetation. The young lad, who thought his companion suspicious, asked why he smiled at the flowers. The old man rushed to hush the lad, saying that it was nothing.

During their meal, the youth got the old man drunk, and after a while, he repeated his question.

The old man, warmed with wine, started his tale. "It was a long time ago. One day I killed a Chechen man, with a dagger, on this very road. When he was dying, he asked the flowers and grass to witness his death. But can they talk? I found it funny then, and I laughed. Indeed, it has been thirty years, but the flowers still bloom like before, and the grasses still grow as tall as a man, as if nothing had happened."

The young lad glanced at the old man and frowned. Then, his eyes shooting fire, he grabbed his dagger. Frightened, the old man fell to his knees and begged for mercy, lamenting about his lonely fortune. In a few more seconds the murderer would finally be punished. The avenged spirit of the poor victim would find peace; what he had wished for thirty years ago would come true. The dagger was high, but the youth suddenly had a thought that had never occurred to him before. The punishment had already caught up to the old man; the secret was out. There was no need to shed blood again.

"Father, your spirit is avenged. Rest in peace," the young lad said. Then he sheathed his dagger and continued on his path.

Tursynbai finished his parable. Khasenkhan invited his silent friends to the 'dastarkhan' (feast).

CHAPTER 5
SOCIALISM AND ITS SHADOW

Conversations about Socialism's history still continue, and I believe they will not quiet down anytime soon. People are looking for a way out of the world financial crisis, and for some reason, they circle back to the idea of Socialism, to the legacy of Karl Marx. It is a very dangerous route, fraught with consequences. Perhaps there is some reason for this phenomenon. If so, what is it? Why do we speak of Socialism more and more often? Keep in mind that people are often not willing to trouble themselves with serious contemplations and discussions because it is much easier to live with an already established stereotype. Besides, they need a quick result. In many cases, there has emerged a strong urge for a specific result. Under Socialism, orders came from above, and the masses had to carry them out without thinking twice or dwelling upon the details. A habit to set goals for others, but not for yourself, has lately gained a strong foothold in the history of humankind. Unfortunately, this habit was installed along with liberal and democratic methods. It may have first occurred in France. Later, it became a global social movement.

At first, we socialized human existence; then we turned it into a political spectacle. Socialism originated from this message but immediately embarked upon solving complex social problems. Communists made it their goal to measure the immeasurable. It was a waste of time. A person's life is his or her personal business. The Kazakh say, "The most important wealth is your health." It is the main principle of life for Muslims. In European countries, democracy created many public, social, and democratic institutes that went on to study and meddle in the personal and private life of each individual, with zest. At that time, Karl Marx developed a theory that surplus value after production costs was exploitation of people by people. The actual situation is somewhat different, and perhaps it requires other measures in the process of socialization and further politicization of human life.

Max Weber had interesting thoughts on this matter. Whenever the conversation drifts into the necessity of changing the order to improve human life, it is bound to mention revolutionary transformations. I believe that is where the root of trouble is hidden. A revolution breaks one and all and establishes new forms of existence and human society. It is a sheer delusion. Half of all humanity was trapped in it. The results were not long in arriving: millions of people died, and the revolutionary press harmed and crushed the fates of several generations. Socialism showed a picture of a good life to people, but Bolsheviks' fairy tales were not new. People already had cherished memories of legends, tales, and biblical stories about life in paradise.

Communists inverted myths in an attempt to prove that heavenly life was possible on earth. Certainly, such a possibility attracted the masses, who believed that paradise on earth was possible, and who plunged themselves into a reckless faith in the new theory of Socialism. People's memories still retain some shreds of that old consciousness. As soon as people encounter difficulties, they immediately remember how good life was under Socialism. According to established opinion, Socialism was a lifesaver for those who feared personal responsibility and strived to shift the load onto somebody else's shoulders. People are used to blaming anyone but themselves for their troubles, and that is a vivid manifestation of irresponsibility, as if all ills are someone else's fault. It is easier to condemn others, and it is more convenient to look at the other side for those at fault.

If you do not have a craft or an education, you cannot provide for your own children. Is it really the fault of the society, state, or authorities? Blaming others, but not yourself, has consequences, and rather undesirable ones. It is to the advantage of those who dream of power to obtain a high position and benefits. In order to take advantage of an explosive situation, they come up with different theories and teachings, one of which is the idea of Socialism. Communists shouldered a disabling burden. Their mistake was neglecting the experience of the past. Nothing they attempted to install corresponded with human nature; they took people's freedoms.

Their promised new life turned into tragedy for the people.

Reflections

When people start talking about Socialism, they always say that everyone was equal under Socialism. Yes, there were many speeches about equality, but they were all a political trick. In reality, there can be no equality among people because every individual is unique; there is no alternative. Take, for instance, a professor and a street cleaner, a poet and an entrepreneur. If we tried to claim that they were equal, it would indicate our neglect of God's creation. He prepared a special and individual fate and life for each person. It is a sin not to seize God-given opportunities.

Therefore, we must distinguish between the equality of people and the equality of their rights. The latter is associated with a democratic society. Justice is about people understanding their destiny and their inability to be exactly the same as others, as well as about the creation of appropriate social conditions.

Advocates of Socialism occasionally admonish current authorities, claiming there is more distress and devastation now than there was then. It is a fact, but it is not the truth. Yes, Bolsheviks in their day provided an adequate salary to everyone, apportioned so that none would starve and none would get wealthy. Indeed, people did not starve; orphans and widows received benefits and aid. The Party knew that, if it were otherwise, they would lose people's trust. That very adherence to the principle of social assistance helped the Party rise in the esteem of common people. The nation continued to live in poverty, but people had clothes to wear, food to eat and drink, and they were happy and grateful for that.

Under Socialism, a creative approach to work disappeared. People stopped striving to master the latest technologies that could increase labor productivity. The quality of manufactured products gradually decreased, quantity took priority over quality. That was mainly because the reduction in quality was convenient and profitable in some facilities; output of low-quality products became a tradition; it became normal. Because of the preservation of jobs and the production of low-quality goods in large quantities, we had no unemployment. Unemployment would have been natural with the use of the latest technology or the implementation of automation. The drive to eliminate unemployment at any cost led to the rise of many idlers and low-quality specialists. It became customary to appoint incompetent officials to high positions. Despite the seeming paradox, such appointments were advantageous to the state because it was easier to deal with such people; they were compliant, agreed to everything, and did not bring up any major problems. They were content with their positions and feared losing them. Such workers were characterized by a desire to avoid any changes; whereas, the ability to maintain the appearance of active work and nominal fulfillment of duties was most welcome.

Intellectuals, in the years of Socialism, were also suppressed and felt constrained. A one-size-fits-all approach was actively introduced into education. Students' potential abilities and intelligence levels were disregarded. One program, one set of requirements, was developed for everyone. In education and in science, quantity and not quality was the governing factor.

In all spheres of human existence, Socialism accepted poor quality and egalitarianism. Therefore, society was infected with a dangerous disease. No matter how much some tried to conceal it, Socialism still revealed its historical feebleness.

****

Socialism is a disease that starts with everyday life. Communist propaganda and campaigning infected millions of people with this disease. The greatest bitterness is that many people, honest and pure in heart, believed in the ideas of Socialism. They believed childishly—completely and sincerely. Later when they discovered the deceit, they broke down and fell into depression. Those who could not part with old stereotypes and ideals are still nostalgic for the return of Socialism.

Curing this disease is a very hard and complicated process. I fear that even the change of generations will not free us from the consequences of the past. Any generation may develop adherents to Socialist ideas. Socialism did indeed exist in the history of human society; it was a global-level phenomenon; its images are embodied in different forms of art. There is always some interest in any type of disease, and creative people often choose the period of Socialism as their topic of pursuit, thereby advocating it, either willingly or unknowingly.

Some see the ideas of Socialism as a game, with a certain grain of irony. Others believe that the ideas were misinterpreted and implemented in the wrong time. They try to modernize its basic principles and reanimate its ideas, but it seems that Socialism offers nothing but menace. Socialism is demonism, and demonism is ineradicable. That is the gravest jeopardy!

Are we who once lived under Socialism to blame? If so, what should be our redemption? Perhaps, we can console ourselves by asserting the inevitability of fate? If the guilt does not escalate to a crime, is forgiveness then possible? What about those who committed crimes—how do they live on? There are no specific and precise answers to these questions.

When the conversation steered into this topic, the elderly Beysen brightened up and readily told me tales of his life. This time again, he let out a heavy sigh and started his story.

The Elderly Beysen's Story

I committed a grave crime: I took a God-given life. It is the most terrible thing that could have happened.

I pray in the mosque every Friday, and it is excruciating for me. Every time I kneel on the ground, I watch other people bowing, and I see criminals like me in them. Otherwise, why do they pray so zealously? What are they asking for from the Creator? Perhaps I see others that way because I committed an evil deed. But I keep scrutinizing the faces of those offering prayers, and I try to determine who may be a criminal.

With a desire to console myself, I say, "Thank you, Lord. I am not the only criminal here."

For me, religion—and even life itself—is only a mirage, an illusion. I am in the same undefined state. It has occurred to me that a crime is something that floats in the air and can attach itself to anyone. It seems to be searching for a suitable person. That is how it got hitched to me. Many years have passed since then; it is long forgotten now. But there I am, just past fifty, and it came back into my memories again, into my life, and there is no escaping it.

I will tell you how it came to me.

I was employed in Solovki prison camp in northern Russia during the Stalinist purges of the 1930s.[22] We were guarding political prisoners then. We took them to work and brought them back. Sometimes we would hold exercises, but mainly we worked as guards.

I recognized him right away. It was my mother's brother, a close relative. I almost rushed to him, wanted to call out to him, but then I remembered that they had warned us, "If you see a relative or someone you know among the prisoners, report it to the counterintelligence department immediately."

---

[22] See esp. Steven A. Barnes, *Death and Redemption: The Gulag and the Shaping of Soviet Society* (Princeton, NJ: Princeton University Press, 2011) and Anne Applebaum, *Gulag: A History* (Doubleday 2003).

I knew what would happen to me in that case: I would get arrested and end up in a prison cell.

When my uncle was passing by, he whispered under his breath, "My boy, we do not know each other. I don't know you, you don't know me."

My colleague Sergey noticed my bewilderment and dismay and poked me in the ribs, "Hey, what's up with you?"

"No, nothing, everything is fine," that was all I could answer.

The platoon sergeant major was a real animal. At first, I reached out to him, happy to see another Kazakh, but then I tried to stay away from him. He had invented his own method for torturing prisoners, which he cynically called a "walk in the fresh air." A victim, stripped to the waist, would be brought outside and tied to a pole. In Solovki, with nothing but wetlands and swamps around, gnats and mosquitos swarmed in multitudes. It was horrible to watch the sufferings of a man completely covered with them. But the sergeant major was not satisfied with that. Every ten or fifteen minutes, he made us fan the victim with branches to shoo away insects that were full of blood and make room for new ones.

It was hard to image what that person felt, what fiendish torments he endured. As I would pass by and see a body, red and swollen beyond recognition, I would try to help, at least in some way. With a gag in his mouth, the poor sufferer could not say anything, but his eyes would be filled with pain as he waited for rescue from the torture.

We did not know whose method the sergeant major had adopted, but they said it had been used since olden times.

One day it was my nagashi's turn. When I saw that the sergeant major was going to send him for some "fresh air," I rushed to the officer, "Listen, there are only three of us Kazakhs in here. Take pity on him; he has done nothing wrong."

He flew into a rage, "Hey, you need to stop your nationalistic nonsense. I have to break him; he's getting too restive. You never know, he might instigate a riot and encourage others to do so, too. Just look into his eyes; he's a real trouble maker."

Yes, the nagashi was a proud and brave man. If he looked into your eyes, you would quickly look away because he was a nobleman in his spirit and in his blood. As a kid, I wanted to be like him.

"Comrade Sergeant Major, I beg you to let him go. He won't do it again," I pleaded.

He stared at me viciously, "All right, then you take a walk in his place."

I had not expected that. "So be it," I thought, and aloud I said, "All right, I agree."

The sergeant major was struck by my answer and burst into a guffaw. It was hard to make out whether it was laughter or roar.

"Okay, be ready by the evening then," the sergeant major said.

Deep in my heart I still thought and hoped that he would not do it.

But in the evening, after dinner, he came up to me, "So, hero, go ahead and strip down."

At that moment I thought about his mother: Did she know what scum she had given birth to?

They put a gag in my mouth, took off my clothes, and tied me to a tree. Gnats and mosquitoes fastened upon me; the pain was infernal. I could hardly breathe; I was bound so tightly I could not move. My eyes swelled so I could not see anything. Mosquitoes were in my nose, on my lips. I must have been unconscious for a while; when I woke up I heard noise and yelling in the barracks. Suddenly, men ran up to me; some cut the ropes, while others whisked away the mosquitos.

"What a bastard," they whispered through clenched teeth.

Later I found out that Sergey, the platoon sergeant, held an old grudge against the sergeant major. When he found out about what had happened, he had attacked the sergeant major, and the others had joined in, forcing an end to my torture.

I spent two days in the medical unit. I did not talk to the sergeant major, but only quietly followed his orders. It would have been all right, but he took my nagashi "for a walk" anyway. The poor man spent an hour covered in gnats. Limp and swollen beyond recognition, he was returned to the barracks. In impotent rage, I clenched my fists, feeling sorry for my nagashi. He fell ill from the insect bites and was sent to the medical unit. I do not know what happened with him after that, whether he survived or perished. Perhaps he asked to be transferred to another camp to spare me torment, I do not know.

After a year of military service, I was promoted to sergeant. Days dragged one after another, monotonous and dull. New "enemies of the people" replaced the dead ones. I wondered where they found all those enemies of the people. The conveyor belt of death was constantly in motion; some died, only to be replaced by others.

Once a month, new prisoners arrived by train. One day, the sergeant major, Sergey, and I all went together to get them. That time the prisoners looked good; they wore dressy clothes, but their eyes showed bewilderment: Where had they been taken? What would they do here?

The sergeant major lined them up and walked back and forth along the line, scrutinizing the newcomers. I knew that he was eager to take those things of theirs that he fancied. We put them in a truck and set off. However, the bridge was washed out, and we had to take a detour. Wetlands and swamps were all around.

Suddenly, the sergeant major ordered the driver to stop. He lined up the prisoners and told them to bag their valuables, watches, and good clothes. The prisoners stayed quiet as they did as they were told. The sergeant major picked up the bag and threw it into the cab.

I noticed that we had stopped right by a swamp. Blood rushed into my head—I suddenly hit the sergeant major on the head with an entrenching tool and dumped him into that swamp.

In a minute or two his head disappeared under the water.

"He that lives wickedly can hardly die honestly. He fell off the truck, straight into the swamp. We had no time to save him," Sergey said firmly.

We reported what had happened to the commanders; everyone confirmed the story.

For a long time, I had forgotten what happened then. But after fifty years, the past has returned to me. I committed a serious crime; I deliberately killed the Kazakh sergeant major. During the long evenings there, I had thought about how to kill my enemy. Then finally, I killed him. If not that time, I would have killed him some other time, some other way. I committed a crime, a terrible violence; I took a man's life. What do I do now?

CONCLUSION

The wider the chasm grows between the rich and the poor, the more the nostalgia for Socialism appears.

How do we resolve that problem? It is a very complicated question. Humanity struggles to find answers to it. Many theories and social practices have been created, but up till now, nothing has changed. As of 2012, wealthy America had 10 percent unemployment; in Spain, this index approached twenty percent. That is one side of the problem; the other side is that even with a job, there is not enough money to provide for the family. This means that social protest is increasing, which may lead to revolutions. That is the road to catastrophe. Is there any other solution? Is it conceivable that the rich would voluntarily share their wealth? Certainly not. So how do we put the end to inequality? I believe that one of the solutions is to use tax policy to regulate social equality.

A poor man always dreams of being wealthy, but does a wealthy man think about a poor man? This issue will always stand at our doorstep.

The camp of Socialism has been destroyed. The Soviet Union has collapsed. In 1991, Kazakhstan gained its independence. The Kazakh Soviet Socialist Republic changed its name to the Republic of Kazakhstan. Along with Socialism, the influence of the Communist Party is now history. The Communist Party continues to operate, but it does not have the might it once had. Previously influential Communists now work in other institutions, advocating for other interests. That is why we can say that Socialism indeed turned out to be an illusion.

At the same time, we cannot ignore the fact that ghosts of the past still creep into the lives, minds, and thoughts of those who lived in the years of Socialism. They still live in the world of those Socialist values that they hold dear. If I think about what value Socialism has given me, my answer is that the only value of Socialism that I hold dear is my life. I lived during those times, I grew up, matured, had a family, brought up my children, and thought of the future. I cannot cross it all out; it is my life. Therefore, the value I cannot abandon is my life. To the best of my ability, I have tried to tell you the story of my life in this novel.

Socialism could not pass the test of maturity; capitalism is not in the best shape either. What is ahead for us? There is much said and written about it. Unfortunately, nothing comprehensible, conclusive, and decisive has yet been created. We need to look for new ways, new approaches and ways of thinking. Fairness for both manufacturers and consumers is necessary. That is true, but how to implement that in reality is a difficult question. Nowadays, everything is governed by market relations and free markets. The global financial crisis has come; capitalism is embroiled in crisis as well. The People's Republic of China, where the Communist Party actively protects the interests of consumers, found a solution to this issue by relying on values particular to that nation. However, their example is unlikely to be employed in other countries.

China's difference is especially noticeable now. European or other national standards cannot be used in Chinese life. There are no pressures on consumers in China other than personal ones (e.g., peer pressure, desire for status symbols, etc.). However, Chinese products freely enter the territory of Africa and find market outlets there. Chinese products have flooded the entire world. You can find goods manufactured in China in every nook, on every continent, in any country, no matter how remote. China's political and economic system is also supported by the Chinese lifestyle, their everyday life, traditions, and mindsets, which are based on Confucianism. In order to maintain their national culture, to ensure its further development, they limit the impact of other cultures and values. That principle is followed very strictly. In contrast, the ideologists of Soviet times fought national traditions in every possible way, trying to destroy them. That was their fatal error. Their violence and insults toward nations' carefully guarded spiritual relics, their abuse of centuries-old lifestyles and established worldviews, were turned against Socialism itself and led to its downfall.

Regardless of the topic for conversation, in one way or another, it always touches upon the manufacturer and the consumer. Both parties need fairness; that is clear and unquestionable. However, the problem remains: How do we put this understanding into action?

Lenin was not mistaken in his solution for the problem between manufacturers and consumers. He saw it as the very core of the revolution. He knew the reasons for shedding blood. He worked hard to implement his ideas. The proof of that can be found in his conversation with foreign army colonel Raymond Robins.

"In the second half of March 1918," Robins recalled, "I talked with Lenin in the Kremlin."

He sat at ease in the tsar office, facing me, and asked me a question, "Colonel Robins, are you familiar with the idea of the Russian revolution?"

I did not understand the question.

"What do you mean, Commissioner? I do not understand."

"Do you know the idea that fuels the Russian Revolution?" he asked again.

"Certainly," I replied. "It is surely democracy directed against the tsar."

"No," replied Lenin. "Our idea is the policy of public control over the manufacturers' economy . . ." (*Pravda*, April 21, 1989).

China had established control over the manufacturers but within the concept of "one country, two systems." Mikhail Gorbachev wanted to follow this path as well, but due to a lack of adequate preparation, he could not implement his intentions. However, Deng Xiaoping succeeded in his plans. In his paper "The Grand Chessboard," Zbigniew Brzezinski wrote that, if China swallows Hong Kong without repressions, Deng Xiaoping's formula of "One country, two systems" may change in its second part. That is, it could become "One country, several systems." His words do make some sense, however, for now China follows two systems.

This novel describes the Soviet form of Socialism, whereas other authors may write about other forms and manifestations of it in greater detail. I only sketched the biography of Socialism, as it is my autobiography as well.

How will this novel be perceived by the young generations who have been born in other times, who have never experienced the pressure of Socialism's propaganda?

For them, Socialism is the past—it is history—but they have fathers and grandfathers who witnessed that history, who took part in it. Therefore, I believe that young people, who are only starting their lives, should know what happened.

To the generation that will have to take the state helm in 2030, I say, support the nation and live at the very crest of events. I dedicate my novel to you.

Hakim Abai said some very powerful words about what we should love. According to Abai, we need to love three things.

First, Abai said we should "Love all of humankind, which was created by the love of God." Every man, being God's creation, should love God. That is how we fulfill our duty before him.

Second, he told us to "Love all of humankind as fellow kin." This is connected with one's love for the Creator. The Creator shaped us all with his love. Despite everyone's differences in skin color, eye shape, religions, diversity, and personality, we all have a right to live, to be happy and succeed as people.

Third, Abai instructs us to "Love fairness and equity, as these are the path of truth." Everyone needs fairness. Abai called the desire for fairness "the Path of God." In other words, love for fairness is righteousness. It is the law of the entire universe; it is the harmony of the world.

When and in what society will these three principles of Abai become priorities and standards for people? It is hard to say. Socialism attempted to find an ideal form for human existence on earth, but the society it created was not perfect.

Perhaps, Abai's three principles will become the content for the acme-society. "Acme," in Greek, means mature. The dream of humanity is the mature society. But how do we build it? How do we live in it? These are the eternal questions that confront every new generation. They are the questions that stand above all times and ages.

I was watching the movie *Nikolai Vavilov* when it suddenly occurred to me, "Why did Bolshevism and fascism become global political powers around the same time? Why?"

It has been shown, on multiple occasions throughout history, that a proletarian revolution leads to catastrophes. It is sufficient to recall the political repressions of the Russian revolution during the construction of Socialism in the USSR, and the tragedy of the Cultural Revolution in China.

How could the fire of fascism flare up in the very center of civilization, in Europe, especially in a country like Germany, which has such deep cultural traditions, and bring horror and nightmares, pain and tragedies to so many nations?

How was fascism related to Socialism? Was there a connection between them? Who helped it to acquire such a monstrous power? Some claimed that fascism was created by discontent to Socialism. How much truth is in that?

World War II was in fact an opposition between Socialism and fascism.

Nevertheless, Socialism defeated fascism and prevailed over it. Does that prove the survivability of Socialism or is there a different meaning?

How can we explain the fact that, after its victory over fascism, Socialism soon ceased to exist as well?

Socialism is the society of the poor, and that is why it is dangerous.

The poor may be mistaken and deluded and may follow a false path. The poor are always bitter and revengeful. Such society has no future. Such society easily falls for provocations that lead to bloody tragedies.

The society of the rich and well-off people is a stable society. Clashes between the rich and the poor can never lead to peace, or agreement, or harmony.

There should be a bridge that spans the abyss between them. The name for that bridge is "government." The main responsibility of a government is to prevent an increase in the gap between the rich and the poor—this should be public policy. Otherwise, the poor will search for a solution in Socialism once again.

And that is very dangerous for the unity and wellbeing of the nation.

Bibliography and Recommended Reading

English:

A. Ahat Andican. *Turkestan Struggle Abroad: From Jadidism to Independence.* Haarlem, Netherlands: SOTA, 2007.

Applebaum, Anne. *Gulag: A History.* Doubleday, 2003.

----------. *Red Famine: Stalin's War on Ukraine.* New York: Doubleday, 2017.

Barnes, Steven A. *Death and Redemption: The Gulag and the Shaping of Soviet Society.* Princeton, NJ: Princeton University Press, 2011.

Black, Jeremy M. *The Holocaust: History and Memory.* Bloomington, IN: Indiana University Press, 2016.

Brezinski, Zbigniew. *The Grand Failure: The Birth and Death of Communism in the Twentieth Century.* New York: Charles Scribner's Sons, 1989.

Cubitt, Geoffrey. *History and Memory.* Manchester, England: Manchester University Press, 2007.

Cohen, G.A. *Why Not Socialism?* Princeton, NJ: Princeton University Press, 2009.

Conquest, Robert. *The Harvest of Sorrow: Soviet Collectivization and the Terror-Famine.* Oxford and New York: Oxford University Press, 1987.

----------. *Stalin: Breaker of Nations.* Penguin Books, 1992.

----------. *The Great Terror: A Reassessment.* 40th Anniversary Edition. Oxford and New York: Oxford University Press, 2007.

Cox, Michael, ed. *Rethinking the Soviet Collapse: Sovietology, the Death of Communism and the New Russia.* London and New York: Pinter, 1998.

Dawson, Christopher. *The Dynamics of World History.* Edited by J.J. Mulloy. Wilmington, DE: ISI Books, 2002.

Dolot, Miron. *Execution by Hunger: The Hidden Holocaust.* New York: W.W. Norton & Co., 1987.

Figes, Orlando. *A People's Tragedy: The Russian Revolution, 1891-1924*. New York, NY: Viking, 2007.

Figes, Orlando. *The Whisperers: Private Life in Stalin's Russia*. New York: Metropolitan Books, 2007.

Fitzpatrick, Sheila. *Stalin's Peasants: Resistance and Survival in the RussiA village after Collectivization*. New York: Oxford University Press, 1994.

----------------------. *Everyday Stalinism: Ordinary Life in Extraordinary Times: Soviet Russia in the 1930s*. Oxford and New York: Oxford University Press, 2000.

Fitzpatrick, Sheila and Yuri Slezkine, eds. *In the Shadow of Revolution: Life Stories of Russian Women from 1917 to the Second World War*. Princeton, NJ: Princeton University Press, 2000.

Fremont-Barnes, Gregory. *The Soviet–Afghan War 1979–89*. Oxford: Osprey Publishing, 2012.

Getty, J. Arch and Oleg V. Naumov. *The Road to Terror: Stalin and the Self-Destruction of the Bolsheviks, 1932-1939*. Translated by Benjamin Sher. Updated and Abridged Edition. New Haven, CT: Yale University Press, 2010.

Hellbeck, Jochen. *Revolution on My Mind: Writing a Diary under Stalin*. Boston, MA: Harvard University Press, 2009.

Harrington, Michael. *Socialism: Past and Future*. Arcade Publishing, 2011.

Khlevniuk, Oleg V. *Stalin: New Biography of a Dictator*. New Haven, CT: Yale University Press, 2015.

Keller, Shoshana. *To Moscow, Not Mecca: The Soviet Campaign against Islam in Central Asia, 1917-1941*. Westport, CT: Praeger, 2001.

Kotkin, Stephen. *Magnetic Mountain: Stalinism as Civilization*. Berkeley: University of California Press, 1997.

Le Goff, Jacques. *History and Memory*. Translated by S. Rendall and E. Claman. New York: Columbia University Press, 1992.

Marples, David R. *The Collapse of the Soviet Union, 1985-1991*. Harlow, England and New York, NY: Pearson/Longman, 2004.

Marwat, Fazal-ur-Rahim Khan. *The Basmachi Movement in Soviet Central Asia: A Study in Political Development*. Pakistan: Emjay Books International, 1985.

Mikhajlov, Valerii. *The Great Disaster: Genocide of the Kazakhs*. Translated by Katharine Judelson. London: Stacey International Publishers, 2013.

Newman, Michael. *Socialism: A Very Short Introduction*. Oxford and New York: Oxford University Press, 2005.

Otteson, James. *The End of Socialism*. Cambridge: Cambridge University Press, 2014.

Privratsky, Bruce. *Muslim Turkistan: Kazak Religion and Collective Memory*. London and New York: Routledge, 2001.

Russian General Staff, *The Soviet-Afghan War: How a Superpower Fought and Lost*, tr. and ed. Lester W. Grau and Michael A. Gress. Lawrence, KS: University Press of Kansas, 2002.

Service, Robert. *Stalin: A Biography*. Boston, MA: Belknap Press, 2006.

Shenk, David. *Global Gods: Exploring the Role of Religions in Modern Societies*. Herald Press, 1995.

Smith, Paul. *Khidr in Sufi Poetry: A Selection*. CreateSpace, 2012.

Snyder, Timothy. *Bloodlands: Europe between Hitler and Stalin*. New York: Basic Books, 2010.

Sowell, Thomas. *A Conflict of Visions: Ideological Origins of Political Struggles*. New York: Basic Books, 2007.

Suny, Ronald. *The Soviet Experiment: Russia, the USSR, and the Successor States*. Oxford and New York: Oxford University Press, 2010.

Tucker, Robert C. *Stalin in Power: The Revolution from Above, 1928-1941*. New York: W. W. Norton & Co., 1990.

Yurchak, Alexei. *Everything Was Forever, Until It Was No More: The Last Soviet Generation*. Princeton, NJ: Princeton University Press, 2005.

Zubok, Vladislav M. *A Failed Empire: The Soviet Union in the Cold War from Stalin to Gorbachev*. Second Edition. Chapel Hill, NC: University of North Carolina Press, 2009.

Kazakh and Russian:

Омарбеков Талас. *Зобалаң*. Алматы, "Санат" 1994 ж.

Омарбеков Талас. *20-30 жылдардағы Қазақстан қасіреті*. Алматы, "Санат" 1997 ж

Қойгелдиев Мәмбет, Омарбеков Талас. *Тарих тағылымы не дейді?* Алматы, "Ана тілі" 1993 ж.

Қойгелдиев Мәмбет. *Алаш қозғалысы*. Алматы, "Санат" 1995 ж.

Қозыбаев Манаш. *"Ақтаңдақтар ақиқаты"*. Алматы, "Қазақ университеті" 1992 ж.

Қозыбаев Манаш. *Тарих зердесі*. Алматы, "Ғылым" 1998 ж.

Назарбаев Нұрсұлтан. *Тарих толқыныда*. Алматы, "Атамұра" 1999 ж.

Назарбаев Нұрсұлтан. *Әділеттің ақ жолы*. Алматы, "Қазақстан" 1991 ж.

Махат Д. *Қазақ зиялыларының қасіреті*. Алматы: "Сөздік-Словарь", 2001 ж.

Тәтімов Мақаш. *Қазақ әлемі*. Алматы, "Атамұра" 1993 ж.

Ғарифолла Есім. *Саяси философия*. Алматы, "Елорда" 2009 ж.

Гарифолла Есим. *«Философия независимости»* Алматы, «Білім» 2011 г.

Аспендияров Санжар. *Қазақстан тарихы*. Очерктер. Алматы, 1994 ж.

Хаин Оралтай. *"Елім-ойлап" өткен өмір*. Алматы, "Білім", 2005 ж.

Шубин Александр. *Социализм. «Золотой век» теории* – 2007 г.

Туган-Барановский М.И. *В поисках нового мира: Социалистические общины нашего времени* – Москва, 1913 г.

Исаев Андрей Алексеевич. *Индивидуальность и социализм*. СПб.: «Кн. маг. А.Ф.Цинзерлинга» – 1907 г.

Богданов Александр Александрович. *Вопросы социализма: Работа разных лет* 2-е изд.-Москва: «Политиздать», 1990

Богданов Александр Александрович. *Что такое социализм? Из истории и теории социализма* – изд. «И.Р.Белопольского»1917 г.

Шеффле Альберт Эбехард. *Сущность социализма* – СПб: «Работник» и "Громади" 1881 г.

Чубайс Игорь Борисовивич. *Россия в поисках себя* – М. : Изд-во НОК "Музей бумаги", 1998

Герберт Спенсер *«Справедливость»* Санкт-Петербург, изд-во: « А. Пороховщикова» 1898 ж.

Карл Поппер. *Открытое Общество и его враги*. Т1,2 Москва Феникс 1992 г.

Хайек Фридрих. *Дорога к рабству*. Астрель, Полиграфиздат, 2012

Людвиг фон Мизес. *Бюрократия. Запланированный хаос. Антикапиталистический ментаьность*. Изд-во: «Дело», 1993

Бакунин М.А. *Федерализм, социализм и антитеологизм*. Петербург-Москва: Книгоиздательство "Голос труда" , 1920.

Фромм Эрих. *Здоровое общество*. Изд. «АСТ», Санкт-Петербург, 2015.

Густав Ле Бон. *Психология социализма*. Изд. «Энграм», Харьков, 1997.

Познер Владимир. *Прощание с иллюзами*. Изд. «АСТ», Санкт-Петербург, 2012.

www.ingramcontent.com/pod-product-compliance
Lightning Source LLC
Chambersburg PA
CBHW020653300426
44112CB00007B/358